Project Editor Nicole Reynolds
Senior Designer Anna Formanek
Additional design LS Design:
Sadie Thomas, Samantha Richiardi
Production Editor Marc Staples
Senior Production Controller Lloyd Robertson
Managing Editor Paula Regan
Managing Art Editor Jo Connor
Publishing Director Mark Searle

Written by Christian Glücklich and Julia March

Inspirational builds created by CEa_TIde/Cyana,
Dominik Senfter, enzo_frsh/Enzo Fischer, Frost_
Beer, Jérémie Triplet, Jonathize, Malte Honsell,
MinecraftRepro/Guillaume Dubocage, Ruben Six,
MYodaa/Hugo, Max Briskey, Jakob Grafe, Sander
Poelmans, sonja firehart, Spritzu, Erik Löf,
Swampbaron, Christian Glücklich
Renders by Swampbaron
Minecraft build project manager Christian Glücklich
Minecraft build project assistant KrimsonBOI
Technical support Maximilian Schröder

DK would like to thank: Jay Castello, Kelsey Ranallo,
Lauren Marklund, Sherin Kwan, and Alex Wiltshire at
Mojang; Catherine Saunders and Lara Hutcheson for
editorial assistance; Julia March for proofreading;
and Kayla Dugger for Americanizing.

First American Edition, 2024
Published in the United States by DK Publishing,
a division of Penguin Random House LLC
1745 Broadway, 20th Floor, New York, NY 10019

Page design copyright © 2024
Dorling Kindersley Limited
20 21 22 23 24 10 9 8 7 6 5 4 3 2 1
001–339555–Sep/2024

A catalog record for this book
is available from the Library of Congress.
ISBN 978-0-5938-4389-5

DK books are available at special discounts when
purchased in bulk for sales promotions, premiums,
fund-raising, or educational use. For details, contact:
DK Publishing Special Markets,
1745 Broadway, 20th Floor, New York, NY 10019
SpecialSales@dk.com

Printed and bound in China

www.dk.com
Minecraft.net

MIX
Paper | Supporting
responsible forestry
FSC™ C018179

This book was made with Forest
Stewardship Council™ certified
paper—one small step in DK's
commitment to a sustainable future.
Learn more at www.dk.com/uk/
information/sustainability

MINECRAFT
FESTIVE IDEAS

Written by Christian Glücklich and Julia March

CONTENTS

BUILDING TIPS

With over 800 blocks to play with and more being added with every update, all it takes is an idea to get creative in Minecraft. In this book, you'll find more than 50 fun, festive ideas. Before you embark on your Minecraft adventure, here are some tips for getting started on a holiday build.

BASIC BLOCKS

Minecraft blocks are your primary festive building materials and are available in lots of different types, such as wood and stone. Many blocks are available as blocks, stairs, slabs, and walls.

BLOCK

STAIRS

WALL

TRAPDOOR

BUTTON

SLAB

REDSTONE BLOCKS

These special blocks allow you to create merry machines and functioning devices. They can be used to build an opening cracker, a moving minecart, and much more.

REDSTONE DUST

POWERED RAIL

REDSTONE

DISPENSER

PISTON

TARGET BLOCK

JOLLY COLORS

Blocks in traditional holiday colors such as red, white, green, and gold are perfect for festive builds. You can also use brightly colored glazed terracotta for presents and wrapping paper.

SNOW

LIGHT BLUE WOOL

BLUE ICE

LIGHT BLUE GLAZED TERRACOTTA

WHITE WOOL

MAGENTA WOOL

RED WOOL

RED GLAZED TERRACOTTA

LIME WOOL

GREEN WOOL

GOLD

YELLOW GLAZED TERRACOTTA

INTERACTIVE BLOCKS

Interactive blocks, also known as utility blocks, have a purpose other than for building. They could be a furnace for cooking winter meals or a cozy bed for guests in an ice hotel.

LEVER

BUTTON

BED

CRAFTING TABLE

CHEST

FURNACE

TRY THIS

The models in this book are here to inspire you. Get creative and personalize your builds. Discover cool ideas for each build in the Try This and Build Tip sections.

SNOWBALL ARENA

Do you like a snowball fight? Build this arena, gather some friends, decide the rules, and challenge them to a snowy tournament as the cheering spectators watch on. Wreaths will add a festive touch to your arena, but don't even think about adding anything warm or cozy. Crackling fires and snowball fights don't mix!

Place stairs upside down to create window arches.

Place spruce leaves in a circle to build a wreath.

Use a shovel to break snow blocks to mine snowballs.

Fill chests with snowballs to snow-verwhelm your opponents in battle!

CIRCULAR ARENA

Create a battle arena in the shape of a snowball. Build a round stadium so spectators are able to see all the action and there are less places for the players to hide!

Decorate the floor of the arena with a snowflake pattern.

Add piles of snow blocks for the players to use for cover.

SPECTATOR PLATFORM

The spectator area is an ideal place for friends to cheer players on. Build a wide viewing platform with wooden planks high above the arena and add a ladder to climb up.

Construct tall walls for the spectators to hide behind during the battle.

Place hoppers around your roof to add a finishing touch.

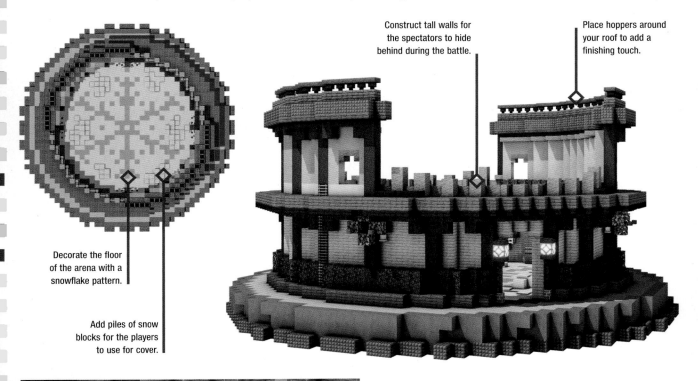

FESTIVE FIGHTERS

Distract hostile mobs away from the snowball fight by adding snow golems. They can throw snowballs at the mobs but can't do any damage. Bring a snow golem to life by placing a carved pumpkin on top of two snow blocks.

TRY THIS

Decorate large walls in your arena with cool pixel art. Use white blocks to create a snowflake image like the design on the floor, or try building a festive check pattern.

ICE PALACE

Still need plans for New Year's Eve? No worries! Just build this magnificent Minecraft ice palace and invite your friends to the coolest end-of-year bash ever. With a venue like this it's bound to be a fancy party, so make guests welcome with a grand ice bridge to cross and lanterns to light their way. Play your blocks right and you might even attract some royal revelers!

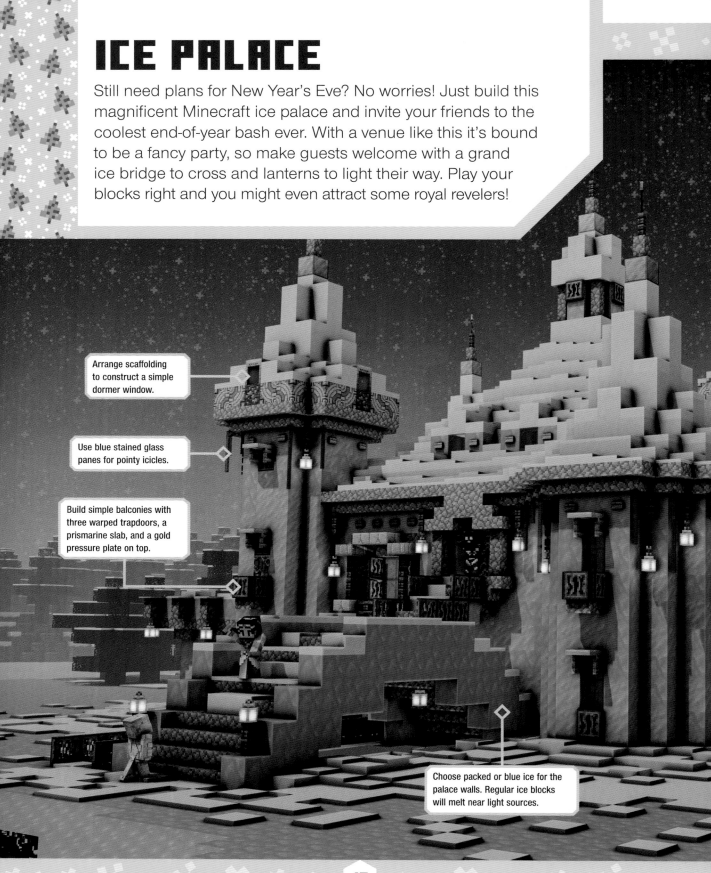

Arrange scaffolding to construct a simple dormer window.

Use blue stained glass panes for pointy icicles.

Build simple balconies with three warped trapdoors, a prismarine slab, and a gold pressure plate on top.

Choose packed or blue ice for the palace walls. Regular ice blocks will melt near light sources.

Top your grand towers with an unlit yellow candle.

Place a few gold blocks to add some royal opulence to your castle.

Use buttons to add extra details to the walls.

BUILD TIP

You're going to need a lot of different types of ice for this frozen palace. In Survival mode, you can use nine ice blocks to craft a packed ice block. Then use nine packed ice blocks to create a blue ice block.

MAJESTIC TOWERS

Towers not only add grandeur and importance to palaces, they also offer great views. These snow-covered roofs look suitably festive, too.

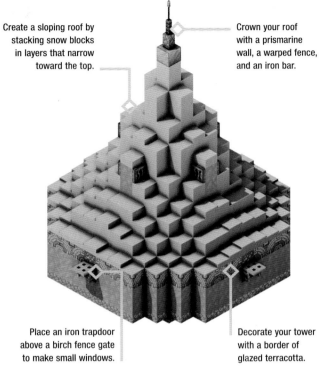

Create a sloping roof by stacking snow blocks in layers that narrow toward the top.

Crown your roof with a prismarine wall, a warped fence, and an iron bar.

Place an iron trapdoor above a birch fence gate to make small windows.

Decorate your tower with a border of glazed terracotta.

GRAND BRIDGE

Build a cool bridge for your ice palace so you can see who's coming to visit. It will also help protect your palace from hostile mobs, who are not welcome!

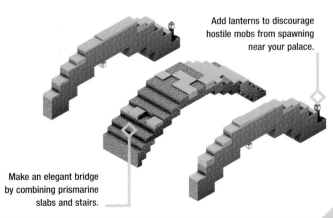

Add lanterns to discourage hostile mobs from spawning near your palace.

Make an elegant bridge by combining prismarine slabs and stairs.

HOME TREE HOME

Give players the perfect present—a festive tree with a secret base inside. It's the ideal place to hide in Survival mode from any hostile mobs who aren't feeling the holiday spirit! Be careful not to let the outside of your tree give any clues to its warm, snug interior. It's just a very large, brightly lit, and amazingly decorated tree. Right?

Add glowstone lights to keep hostile mobs from spawning.

Bookshelves add a cozy detail to your interiors.

TRY THIS

You could create the walls of this base using leaves instead of concrete. For an additional challenge, grab some shears in Survival mode and harvest all the leaves you need.

Make sure each floor of the base is at least three blocks high so players can walk around.

Use stairs, a ladder, or a bubble elevator to access all levels of your base.

Build your tree in a snowy taiga biome so that it has a winter wonderland backdrop.

LEAFY SURVIVAL BASE

This build needs lots of green blocks, but luckily you can fit all the ones you need in one double chest! It uses 16 stacks of dyed concrete and 15 stacks of lime and green terracotta.

SPIRAL STAIRCASE

A simple ladder would work well inside your tree base, but why not build a staircase with a twist! Spiral staircases not only look elegant, but they also save space.

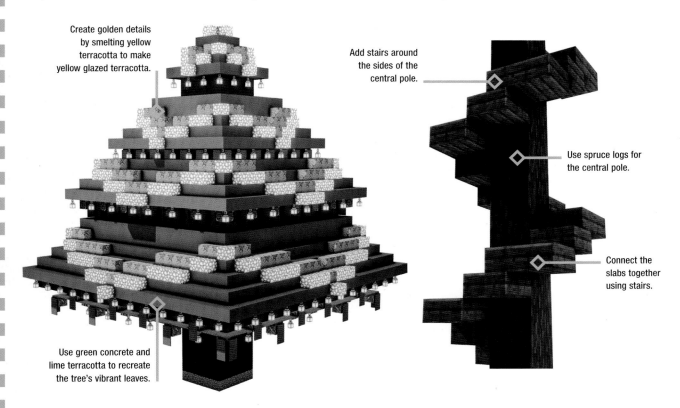

Create golden details by smelting yellow terracotta to make yellow glazed terracotta.

Use green concrete and lime terracotta to recreate the tree's vibrant leaves.

Add stairs around the sides of the central pole.

Use spruce logs for the central pole.

Connect the slabs together using stairs.

ORNAMENTS

Experiment with glazed terracotta, colorful trapdoors, stained glass, and lanterns to make ornaments. They are tree-mendous fun to make and decorate your base with.

LIBRARY

Create a library for your tree base by crafting bookshelves and stacking them into tall library shelves. You could also invite a librarian villager to come and inspect the books.

LANTERN LAUNCH

In winter, cozy lantern festivals are held all around the world to brighten the dark evenings. Launch these colorful lanterns high into the night sky and get players into the festive mood. Once you've brought the spectators out to watch the lantern festival, you'll want to keep them warm and fed, so set up some street food stalls down below. Sweet berries, anyone?

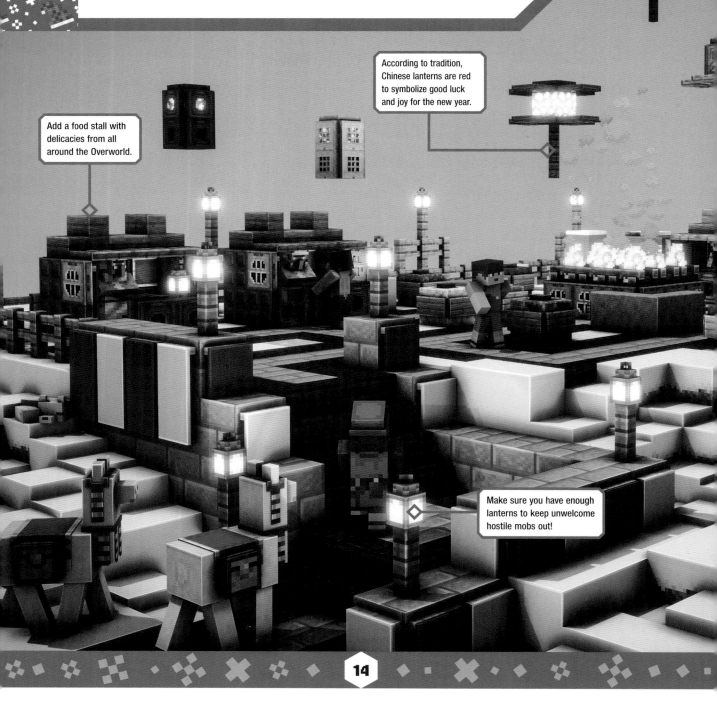

According to tradition, Chinese lanterns are red to symbolize good luck and joy for the new year.

Add a food stall with delicacies from all around the Overworld.

Make sure you have enough lanterns to keep unwelcome hostile mobs out!

Sea lanterns, froglights, and shroomlights can make a great alternative to the glowstone used here.

Add a cozy seating area with chairs made of coral blocks and birch planks.

TOP TIP

Build the festival site on a nearby mountain or hill to have the perfect view of the lanterns. Invite friends to brighten things up with a lantern-building competition.

LANTERNS

These lanterns are simple to recreate. Use different types of wooden trapdoors to make a variety of lantern colors and patterns.

Use crimson trapdoors, fences, and a glowstone block to recreate this lantern.

Close some trapdoors to give the lantern a unique look.

Use bamboo trapdoors for a lattice-patterned lantern.

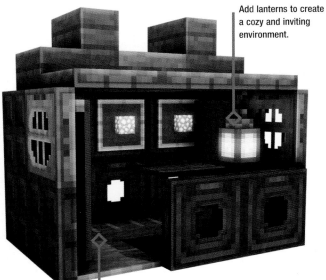

Add lanterns to create a cozy and inviting environment.

Place carpets to give your villagers a soft surface to stand on.

STALLS

Create a variety of stalls for different villager professions and trades. You can decorate each stall to show what the villager is trading inside.

FESTIVE CALENDAR

Can't wait to unwrap your presents? This Minecraft festive countdown calendar will give you something to open every day until it's time. The tall red house has numbered windows, each with a rare item or a tiny seasonal build idea behind them. Candles, presents, winter scenes—it's up to you what festive delights your windows will reveal!

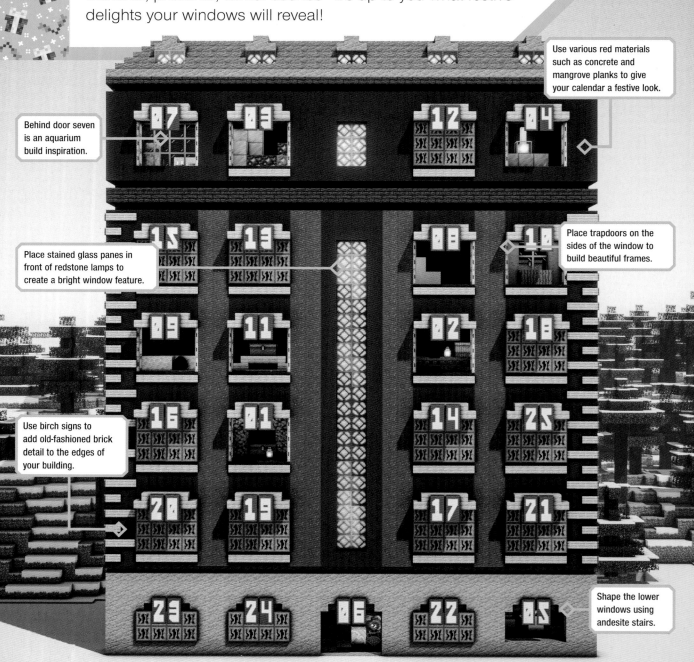

Use various red materials such as concrete and mangrove planks to give your calendar a festive look.

Behind door seven is an aquarium build inspiration.

Place trapdoors on the sides of the window to build beautiful frames.

Place stained glass panes in front of redstone lamps to create a bright window feature.

Use birch signs to add old-fashioned brick detail to the edges of your building.

Shape the lower windows using andesite stairs.

THE CALENDAR

Excitement awaits behind every window on this calendar. Each day, use scaffolding or ladders to reach the window, then open it by removing the trapdoors in front of it.

Close off the windows with colorful trapdoors.

TRY THIS

Add a lantern behind each of the windows. After removing the 24 trapdoors, you will be left with a twinkling festive calendar to use as a decoration on the big day.

NUMBERS BANNERS

Make numbers to count the days up to the 24th. First, craft the banners using wool and sticks. Then use a loom to dye the banners in a specific pattern to create the number.

EPIC LOOT

Place chests and shulker boxes filled with loot behind some windows. Treats for players can include gold, gems, food, or enchanted clothing that would otherwise be difficult to find.

MINI BUILDS

Other windows hide mini builds to provide players with build inspiration for that day. This beacon mini build is fueled by nine shiny gold blocks. You could decide to build a huge pyramid to place the beacon on.

NUTCRACKER SENTRY

Nuts were a favorite festive treat of the Victorians, but they couldn't buy the preshelled ones we have today. They had to crack their own. Build a traditional fierce-faced nutcracker sentry in giant size and let it watch over your wintry biomes. It might not look merry, but with its scarlet coat this nutcracker soldier will certainly look bright.

White concrete and polished blackstone buttons are perfect for making eyes.

Try different placements of stairs and slabs to create unique shapes for beards and hair.

Wool, terracotta, and concrete blocks are perfect for a bright soldier's uniform.

The shoelaces are made of signs placed around the sides and front of the shoes.

Use terracotta variants for the hands and face.

Use oak trapdoors to add texture to the nutcracker's hair.

Stripped dark oak wood and stairs are shaped to look like a lever.

BUILD TIP

Check that the proportions of your build are correct by viewing it from another perspective. Take a big step back and look at your nutcracker statue from every angle before deciding if you are happy with it.

BAUBLE BRIGHT

You've probably seen fabulous glass tree baubles with tiny winter scenes or festive figures inside, but have you ever seen one with a merry Minecraft skeleton? To build this bony bauble, you'll need quartz blocks, stairs, and slabs for the skeleton's body and a lot of glass blocks for the ornament's shell. Be careful not to break any!

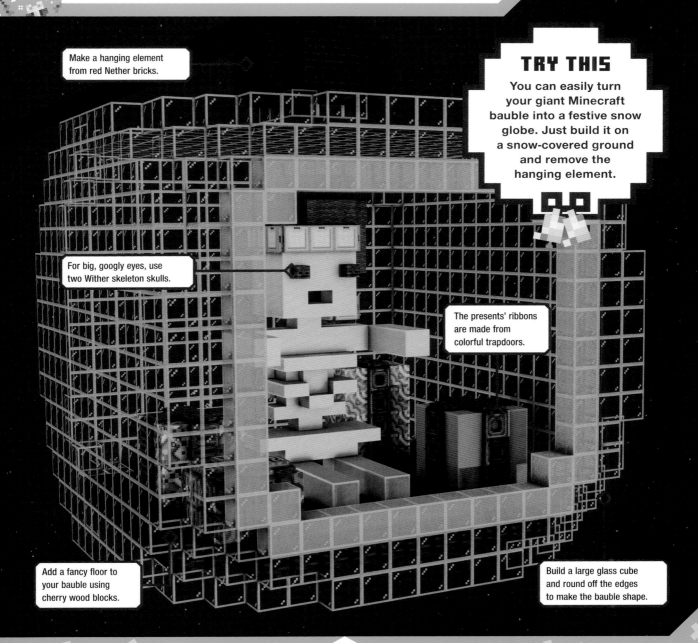

Make a hanging element from red Nether bricks.

TRY THIS

You can easily turn your giant Minecraft bauble into a festive snow globe. Just build it on a snow-covered ground and remove the hanging element.

For big, googly eyes, use two Wither skeleton skulls.

The presents' ribbons are made from colorful trapdoors.

Add a fancy floor to your bauble using cherry wood blocks.

Build a large glass cube and round off the edges to make the bauble shape.

CHRISTMAS MARKET

For last-minute festive shopping, this bustling Minecraft market is the place to be. It's packed with stalls selling food, drinks, and gift ideas galore. Once they've checked off everything on their list, players can relax. Time to skate on the ice rink, or maybe just sit down with a slice of pumpkin pie or two. You did remember to build a pumpkin pie stall, didn't you?

Decorate your stalls with colorful banners.

Add a festive tree (or two) to give the market extra holiday charm.

Build the stalls using stripped spruce logs and other spruce variants, such as slabs, trapdoors, fences, and fence gates.

Pick up some wool at this stall occupied by a shepherd and their loom.

TRY THIS

Use different blocks in similar colors for the market's floor. These gray paths use a mixture of dead coral, stone, andesite, and gravel blocks to create texture.

Connect cobwebs in a garland to look like a chain of snowflakes.

This outdoor seating is made of birch slabs and birch trapdoor backrests.

OUTDOOR FUN

Enjoy the outdoors at this market by sliding across the ice rink or cozying up in the seating area. The rink is 25 blocks long and 12 blocks wide, allowing plenty of space to glide freely away from the Christmas market crowds.

CRAFT CORNER

Building a market takes hard work and creativity. In Survival mode, make a special corner to craft building materials, such as stairs and slabs, that can be sold in your stalls.

Have a grindstone nearby to repair your tools after building the stalls.

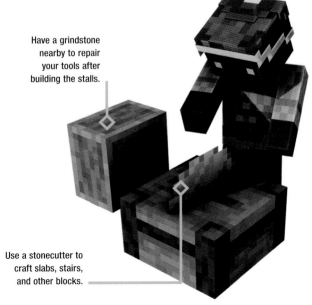

Use a stonecutter to craft slabs, stairs, and other blocks.

FESTIVE CORNERS

As the winter nights close in, it's fun to decorate our homes in preparation for the festivities. You could do the same for your Minecraft house. A festive corner in every room can create a real holiday feel. What best says "winter" to you? A fir tree with lights? Of course! A brightly wrapped present? For sure! A table laden with festive fare? Yes, please!

GIFT CHEST

Build a large, festive gift chest using oak planks and spruce wood. Add dark oak signs for contrast, then fill it with lots of items and colorful presents made from shulker boxes.

Leave the corners of the chest lid empty for a rounded look.

Keep your loot safe with a lock made from polished andesite blocks and stairs.

Top shulker box gifts with carpet. To open the present, you will need to first remove the carpet.

FESTIVE TREE

Create a magnificent festive tree in Minecraft. This one is six blocks high and uses a mud brick wall as a trunk. Adorn it with lit candles and a bright lantern on top.

Decorate the tree with flowering azalea leaves.

Add a glowing lantern as a finishing touch.

Decorate the floor with red and yellow carpets.

HOLIDAY DINNER

Set the mangrove slab table and invite your friends over for a memorable festive dinner. Decorate the dining room walls with a beautiful garland.

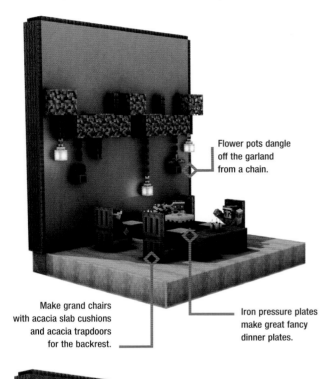

Flower pots dangle off the garland from a chain.

Make grand chairs with acacia slab cushions and acacia trapdoors for the backrest.

Iron pressure plates make great fancy dinner plates.

GIANT PRESENT

Wrap a chest or shulker box in a thick layer of wool to mimic colorful wrapping paper. Make the color of the present hint at the item inside.

Simple bow is made from three yellow wool blocks.

Build strobe lights using End rods and levers.

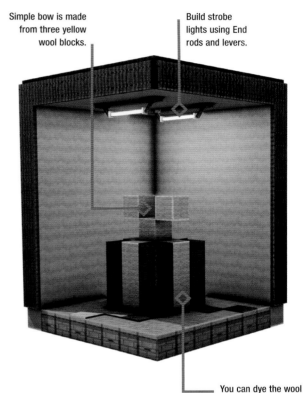

You can dye the wool 16 different colors.

MICRO CITY

Build a festive micro city within a wooden frame. This compact creation is only two blocks deep but still manages to include trees, houses, and a tower.

Build your frame using dark oak trapdoors, slabs, stairs, and spruce signs.

Add buttons to create tiny windows for your micro houses.

TRY THIS

Festive decorations can be made to fit corners of all sizes. Use blocks and items in new ways to enlarge a chest, miniaturize a tree, or build a giant winter scene.

SANTA'S WORKSHOP

Holiday time is super busy for Santa's elves. Right up to the big day, they're hard at work making presents for delivery all over the Overworld. Build a Minecraft version of Santa's workshop with tables, conveyor belts, and lanterns. This wood-beamed workshop might be in a snowy plains biome, but the elves are kept warm by the roaring fire.

Combine a red banner, white dye, and a flower charge pattern on a loom to create this decoration.

Make a traditional-looking fireplace from brick variants.

Single chests have 27 slots for items, so each cart can carry lots of gifts!

Use both dark oak and spruce slabs to create a textured wooden ceiling.

TRY THIS

Instead of building a workshop from scratch, just build it inside a mountain or underground. You won't need to worry about how it looks from the outside or even build a roof.

CONVEYOR BELT

Move goods effortlessly around the workshop using rails and minecarts. Elves can give carts a push to move them from A to B!

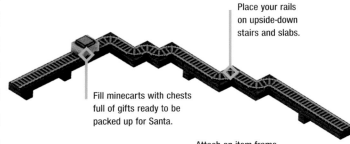

Place your rails on upside-down stairs and slabs.

Fill minecarts with chests full of gifts ready to be packed up for Santa.

Attach an item frame with a cobweb to create a clever ribbon.

GIFT BOXES

Use shulker boxes for small presents. Unlike chests, elves can pick these boxes up with items inside.

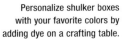

Personalize shulker boxes with your favorite colors by adding dye on a crafting table.

Hang the glazed terracotta blocks from the leaves.

Use fences to support your garland and match the wooden workshop decor.

INDOOR GARLAND

Bring the outside in with this festive garland. Gather leaves with shears and then add additional decoration with colorful glazed terracotta block baubles.

IGLOO HOME

There's no home like a snow home! Pack your bags and build a base in one of the most ice-olated biomes in the Overworld. This dome-shaped domicile is set up for adventurers, with thick walls to keep out the cold and modular rooms filled with supplies. The stray mobs that spawn in the snowy taiga biome will get a frosty welcome here!

Reinforce the walls with iron bars for extra strength.

Place smooth quartz stairs and slabs in a dome shape.

Connect igloo modules to the central biome with polished deepslate.

Build a well from an acacia fence and fence gate, then add chains to a cauldron to make a water receptacle.

Curious snow foxes are passive, friendly visitors.

TRY THIS

Generic igloo structures generate in snowy taiga, plains, and slopes biomes. Find one to use for your base and refurbish it with extra modules, decorations, and warm lighting.

IGLOO MODULES

This igloo has three main modules packed with supplies for an explorer. It has a comfy living room, a magical enchantment space, and a small farm.

Top the igloo with torches to light your way home at night.

Grow pretty flowers on your farm, like blue orchids and torchflowers.

The module's size depends on what's inside. This cozy enchanting space is small, with a low ceiling.

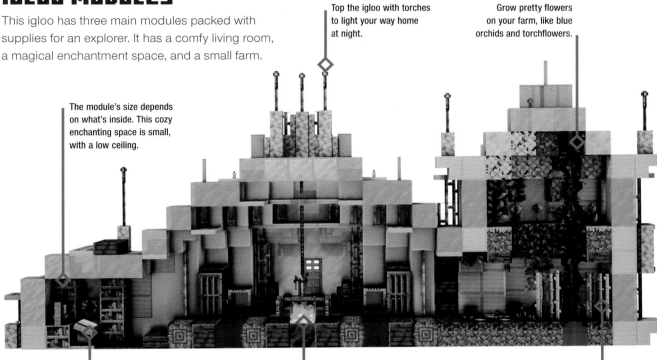

Document your ice adventures using a book and quill.

A soul campfire is useful for an igloo as it doesn't melt snow.

Sugar cane is a useful crop for making sugar and paper.

SHAPED SNOW

To create this igloo, begin by building the largest module in the middle, placing snow blocks in a dome shape. Add modules on each side, with one being the entrance.

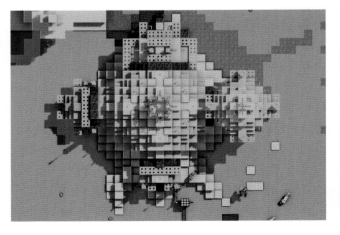

LIVING SPACE

It might be cold and snowy outside, but it can be warm and cozy inside. Sp-ice up your igloo interior with bunk beds made from trapdoors, bookshelves, and a fireplace.

ROAMING REINDEER

Is it going to rain, dear? Not in this snowy plains biome. Snow rules here, and that suits this reindeer family. Players have nothing to fear from these jolly deer. They're only out for a frolic, and maybe to ring in the New Year (or even the new deer—baby Rudolph in the middle). Reindeer are surprisingly big animals, so make your deer family tall and imposing.

Adult reindeer are 19 blocks tall.

Combine two mangrove slabs to create Rudolph's famous red nose.

Use spruce and birch blocks to create the dark and light parts of the reindeer's hair.

Decorate the floor with poppies and dandelion flowers.

TRY THIS

You can make your deer look to the left or right by placing blocks diagonally to angle the neck. Experiment with different angles to make a variety of unique reindeer.

Leave a space between blocks to represent the eyes.

Create cute reindeer hooves using deepslate tile blocks.

ANTLERS

Did you know that reindeer shed and regrow their antlers each year? In Minecraft, you can change or add to them whenever you like, or even have none at all.

These antlers are symmetrical, but yours can point in any direction.

Use dark oak planks and stairs to build pointy antlers.

Add birch blocks to create a lighter-colored neck.

Make the hind leg appear round by placing spruce planks in a cross shape.

Rudolph's neck is made from three blocks placed diagonally.

BABY RUDOLPH

He might be the baby of this family, but Rudolph stands a mighty 15 blocks tall and is made of 360 blocks. He's still a deer little thing though.

Angle the legs to suggest movement.

FESTIVE CAKES

Check out these builds of seasonal cakes from around the world. There's a bûche de Noël (French for Yule log), a strawberry-topped Japanese Christmas cake, and a crispy Australasian pavlova. Yum! You can create these or invent your own. Why not have a Minecraft block-off with your friends and see who can make the tastiest-looking cake?

Add leafy decorations for a festive-looking Yule log.

Create shiny strawberries using red wool and green candles.

Use brown carpets to create an icing-style effect on the cake.

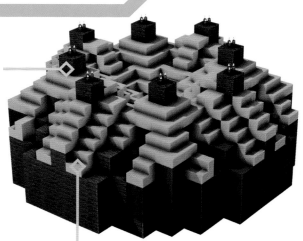

Use smooth quartz stairs to make the frosting look like it's dripping down the sides.

Arrange smooth quartz slabs on top and blocks on the sides to give an all-white meringue look.

Mimic a swirl of cream or white icing with white terracotta or smooth quartz.

BUILD TIP

It's a piece of cake to build tasty-looking baked goods in Minecraft. If you don't know where to begin, first focus on the three key elements of the cake you would like to build, such as log shape, chocolate texture, and icing swirl.

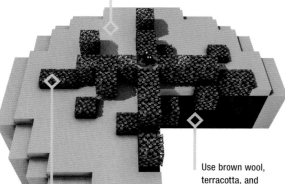

Design a snowflake shape on top using birch leaves to decorate the pavlova.

Use brown wool, terracotta, and concrete to fill the cake's interior.

MICRO HOLIDAY VILLAGE

Who wants a festive break in a Minecraft holiday village?
It'll have to be a mini break, because this build is strictly
microscale. Perfect peace reigns in this pocket-sized scene,
where snowflakes twinkle in the evening lights. Players
will feel like giants among the sprawling micro houses,
tiny town square, and itsy-bitsy ice rink.

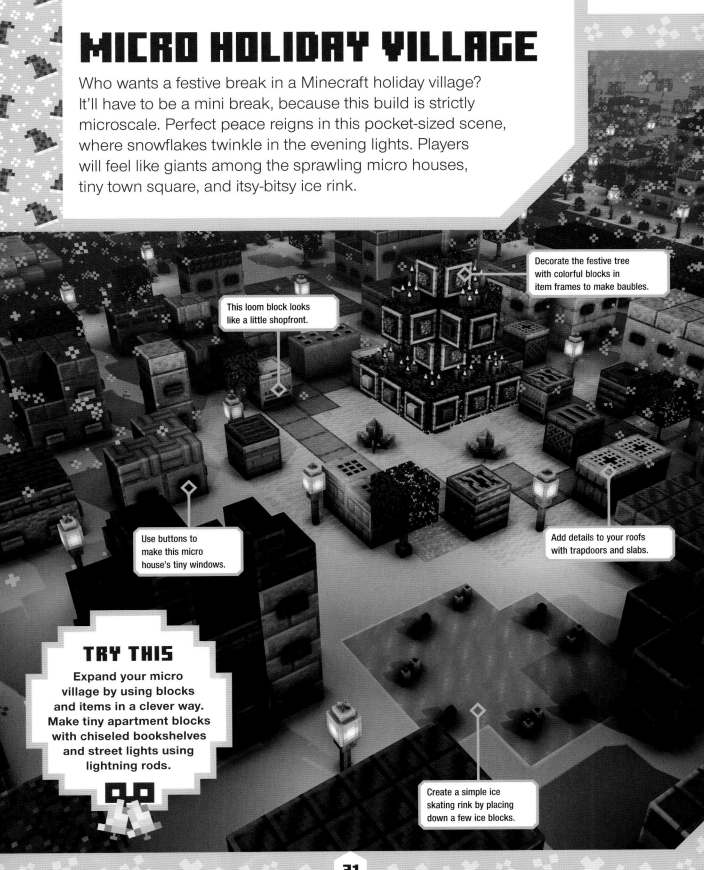

Decorate the festive tree
with colorful blocks in
item frames to make baubles.

This loom block looks
like a little shopfront.

Use buttons to
make this micro
house's tiny windows.

Add details to your roofs
with trapdoors and slabs.

TRY THIS

Expand your micro
village by using blocks
and items in a clever way.
Make tiny apartment blocks
with chiseled bookshelves
and street lights using
lightning rods.

Create a simple ice
skating rink by placing
down a few ice blocks.

SUNNY SOUTHERN HEMISPHERE HOLIDAY

What, no snow? Not in the southern hemisphere—the part of the world that lies below the equator. Holiday time here falls in the summer. Forget log fires and armchairs for this Minecraft build. Players will have more use for beachwear and beach chairs.

Use oak leaves to recreate palm leaves.

Include some tropical flowers, like pitcher plants, to add to the summery, beachy look.

BUILD TIP

Holiday garlands and decorative banners look super festive whatever the weather. Build colorful bunting to hang off the tropical palm trees using red glazed terracotta and white terracotta.

A dual-smoker grill is perfect for a festive barbecue on the beach!

Build festive beach chairs using dark prismarine slabs and stairs, with warped signs as armrests.

Add cocoa beans to look like coconuts.

This small sleigh is made from red Nether bricks and a bamboo underside.

SUN UMBRELLA

Protect Santa from the Sun's rays with a colorful parasol. If you build it big enough, there will be plenty of shade for two!

Add an extra Nether slab in the center for the umbrella's peak.

Combine red Nether brick slabs with smooth quartz slabs for the canopy.

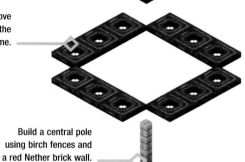

Use mangrove trapdoors for the wooden frame.

Build a central pole using birch fences and a red Nether brick wall.

SMOKEY BBQ

Prepare tasty dishes with this dual-grill BBQ, made of two smokers. Add iron doors as a lid and an iron trapdoor as a side table, perfect for placing food on.

SPOT THE DIFFERENCE

One snowy biome. Two Minecraft builds. They look identical at first glance, but they contain five subtle differences designed to baffle and bamboozle any players you challenge to find them. If you try building a spot the difference challenge, remember to keep a record of the differences. You don't want to end up puzzled by your own puzzle!

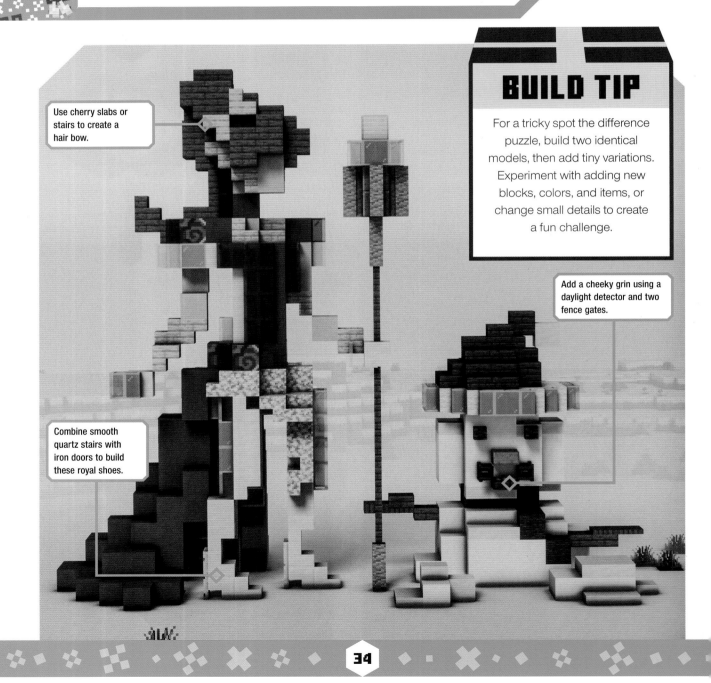

Use cherry slabs or stairs to create a hair bow.

BUILD TIP

For a tricky spot the difference puzzle, build two identical models, then add tiny variations. Experiment with adding new blocks, colors, and items, or change small details to create a fun challenge.

Add a cheeky grin using a daylight detector and two fence gates.

Combine smooth quartz stairs with iron doors to build these royal shoes.

FROSTY FRIENDS

What will you build for your festive spot the difference? This build shows a snow queen with red cape and scepter and her super-cute snowperson companion.

Give your frosty friend a cute red sandstone slab nose.

Place two Wither skeleton skulls for the snowperson's eyes.

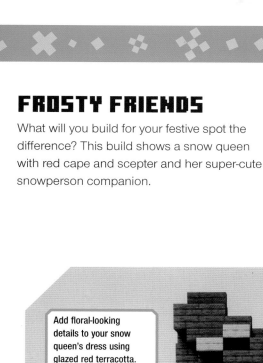

Add floral-looking details to your snow queen's dress using glazed red terracotta.

Build the tip of the scepter from white stained glass panes and iron blocks.

Smooth quartz slabs, white wool, and white stained glass make a fluffy hat trim.

FESTIVE CAROUSEL

Holiday season can be a bit of a whirl, just like a carousel.
This wreath-decked carousel doesn't spin, but building it will
still give you a thrill. Make some Minecraft mounts—perched
on poles like real carousel horses—then set them in a ring
under a red conical roof. Don't forget to add festive lights for
that seasonal glow. Giddy-up and start building!

TRY THIS

To light up the carousel's
roof, connect redstone
lamps with redstone dust
and repeaters in a loop. Then,
to create a circuit, place a
button and press it to
start a dazzling
light show.

Place redstone lamps
and soul lanterns to
light up your carousel.

For great views, build
a viewing platform at
the center of the ride.

Add festive garland decor
made from spruce leaves
and candles.

Create a colorful patterned
floor using copper variants
with a smooth stone outline.

CAROUSEL HORSES

Build carousel horses by combining fences, slabs, stairs, and trapdoors. You could experiment with other animals, too, such as unicorns or giraffes.

CONICAL ROOF

To make a cool conical roof for your carousel, stack colorful blocks in a circle. Make the stacks taller as you build upward to create a sloping cone shape.

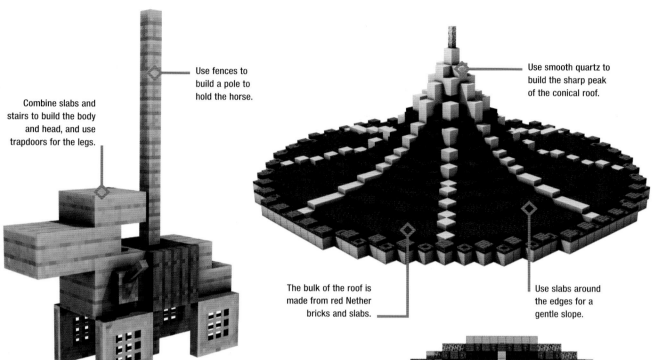

Use fences to build a pole to hold the horse.

Combine slabs and stairs to build the body and head, and use trapdoors for the legs.

Use smooth quartz to build the sharp peak of the conical roof.

The bulk of the roof is made from red Nether bricks and slabs.

Use slabs around the edges for a gentle slope.

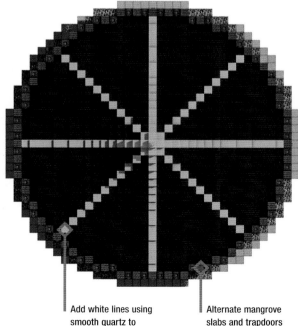

VIEWING PLATFORM

Climb up the ladder to the viewing platform in the middle of the carousel. From there, you can sit on a bench and watch all the players having a great time.

Add white lines using smooth quartz to create a star shape.

Alternate mangrove slabs and trapdoors around the edge.

HIDE-AND-SEEK

Everyone loves the classic game of hide-and-seek. Why not build this Minecraft version with a holiday twist? Players can hide under trees, in buildings, and behind giant candy canes while the seeker tries to find them. If you're the seeker, here's a tip: You know how you're told not to peek inside presents before the big day? This is the one time you can ignore that!

Players can hide behind tall candy canes made of red and white concrete and quartz stairs.

Create presents big enough to hide in from concrete and wool.

Build simple paths from cobblestones, andesite, and diorite.

Plant lots of spruce trees for festive hiding places.

Leave a gap between the floating ice and water for players to hide in the pond.

TRY THIS

Agree on some hide-and-seek rules with your friends before you start. For instance, you could build a fence around your hide-and-seek area to make a clear border.

SURPRISE GIFT

Create a hide-and-seek map with innovative hiding spots, such as inside a large present. Add a secret two-block-high opening in the build for players to sneak into.

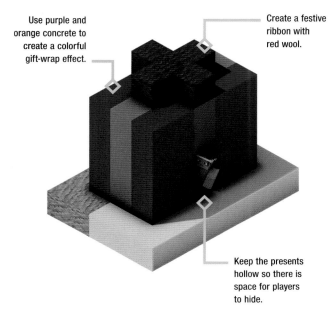

Use purple and orange concrete to create a colorful gift-wrap effect.

Create a festive ribbon with red wool.

Keep the presents hollow so there is space for players to hide.

FESTIVE HIDEOUT

Build a cute festive cabin using wooden planks, logs, and stairs. This hub could be a great place to hide or a perfect spot for the seeker to wait while other players hide.

SNOWPERSON POSSE

If it's not snowing in the real world, you can always build a friendly snowperson in Minecraft. You might not need a hat and scarf, but in a snowy biome, your snowpeople will! Alongside your snowpeople's colorful matching hats and scarves, use brown blocks and slabs for their twiggy arms. Don't forget to add a nose and a row of buttons!

COOL CLOTHES

Keep your snowpeople warm with hats and scarves made from wood and stone variants. Experiment with different color combinations for super stylish snowpeople.

Build a bright bobble hat with red Nether bricks and wool.

Use wooden slabs and stairs to make twiglike arms.

Mix crimson stairs and slabs with cherry wood for this hat with a birch wood brim.

Matching scarf is made from the same materials as the hat.

Signs and stairs make cute buttons.

Create a contrasting hat brim using birch wood.

This round snowperson is 12 blocks wide in the largest area.

BODY BUILDER

To build a snowperson, you will need to make three round sections—a small one for the head, a medium-sized one for the torso, and a larger ball for the base.

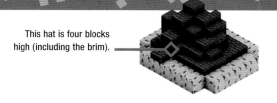

This hat is four blocks high (including the brim).

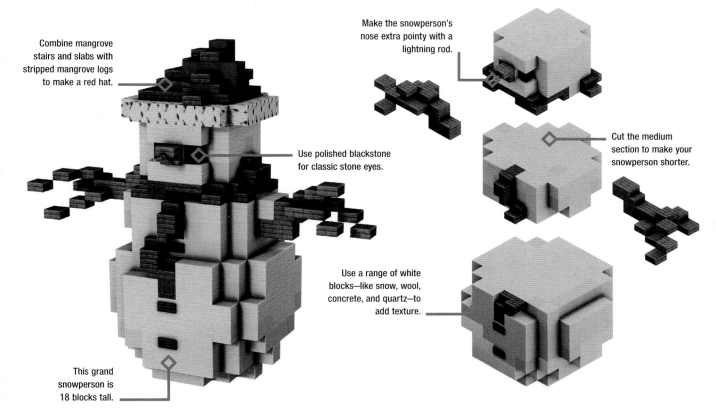

Combine mangrove stairs and slabs with stripped mangrove logs to make a red hat.

Use polished blackstone for classic stone eyes.

Make the snowperson's nose extra pointy with a lightning rod.

Cut the medium section to make your snowperson shorter.

Use a range of white blocks—like snow, wool, concrete, and quartz—to add texture.

This grand snowperson is 18 blocks tall.

BUILD TIP

How is your snowperson feeling? Arrange its face in different ways to convey emotion. Placing the eyes above the nose makes your snowy pal look more cheerful, while positioning the eyes next to the nose makes it look sterner.

SNOWY PUDDLE

The Sun has come out and melted this poor snowperson! Rearrange the blocks used in your snowperson to create this snowy puddle instead.

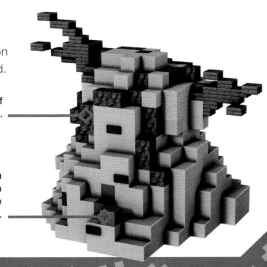

Smooth basalt scarf is still visible.

Add a few stripped acacia logs near the base to show the nose has nearly melted onto the ground.

YULE GOAT

In Scandinavian countries a goat made of straw is a traditional symbol of winter festivities. Most Yule goats are small enough to hang on trees, but this Minecraft one is so big, it can only hang out in an open field. In fact, as Yule goats go, it could be the G.O.A.T.! Build your goat from hay bales, then let it stand proud, ready for other players to admire.

BUILD TIP

Begin building your straw goat by outlining its shape. You can use any materials for this, as they will be covered by the outer blocks. This outline acts as a guide, making it easier to visualize and construct the goat's features.

Use polished blackstone buttons on each side for the goat's eyes.

Use brown blocks like dripstone, packed mud, or wood to create your goat's beard.

Add white stained glass panes to give your goat a covering of ice.

Create contrast and texture against the hay with blocks such as red terracotta and mangrove stairs.

PERKY PENGUIN

Waddle you build next? How about this Minecraft penguin, all black and white and perfectly perky in the snow. Penguins aren't the most graceful birds when they're walking, but this one looks quite dignified as it stands with its egg and surveys its frosty biome. Don't make its wings too large. Penguins are strictly flightless birds, so you don't want to give yours ideas!

Make your penguin a crested penguin by adding a bamboo trapdoor crest.

Build the beak with bamboo slabs, planks, and trapdoors.

Combine black concrete, black wool, and black terracotta for the wings and body.

Penguin's belly is made from white wool and concrete powder.

TRY THIS

With some little tweaks, you can turn your penguin into an adorable house. Replace a few blocks with stained glass to make small windows and add an entrance through the egg.

Make the egg oval using diorite stairs, walls on the sides, slabs below, and iron trapdoors in front.

THE ELF EXPRESS

Santa's workshop is full of activity. The elves must read orders, make and package presents, then get them to the sleigh on time. How do they keep everything on track? With the Elf Express! This powered rail-and-cart system smoothly links all stages of production, banishing bottlenecks and minimizing mix-ups, so you can be sure your present will be delivered.

This workshop uses powered rails that keep the minecarts moving.

Players can hitch a ride by sitting in the minecarts.

TRY THIS

Turn these colorful elf workshop shelves into a practical storage solution. Replace the glazed terracotta blocks with chests and shulker boxes to hold hundreds of items.

Mix jungle planks, slabs, and trapdoors to create rustic shelves.

Add colorful glazed terracotta blocks to the shelves to look like they're full of presents.

Support your rail system with pillars. They can be made of solid blocks or from hollow trapdoors.

Place beehives on the floor for a textured and natural-looking surface.

ELVES' WORKBENCH

Transform your crafting table into a magical workbench. Add stairs on each side and item frames on top to display the elves' current projects.

ELVES NEED A HOLIDAY, TOO

Don't forget that elves also want to celebrate the holidays. Decorate the workshop by adding a green terracotta tree, stained glass leaves, and twinkling candles and lanterns to make sure that the elves feel festive, too.

HOLIDAY MAZE

Left, right, left, left, right ... oh no, it's another dead end! This circular Minecraft maze will have players running this way and that as they try to make it to the central tree in time for a carol concert. Snow-topped hedges and numerous ways to go wrong will confuse anyone taking on this festive-but-frustrating maze. Players who make it through deserve a tasty milk drink.

Add red and green banners on tall fence posts so players can always see where the center is.

Top the tree with a star made from four rotated birch stairs.

Decorate the base of your tree with some colorful gift boxes.

Build your walls using different types of leaves, such as oak and spruce.

Scatter snow layers randomly to create a light dusting of snow.

A-MAZE-ING!

For a circular maze, build a big circle with four smaller ones inside. Open and block paths between the circles to create a challenging route through your maze. For extra difficulty, block some paths with dead ends.

TOWERING TREE

The highlight of the maze is the festive tree, full of colorful decorations. Build the tree wider at the base and narrower at the top. It's okay if it's not perfectly symmetrical—most real-life trees aren't either!

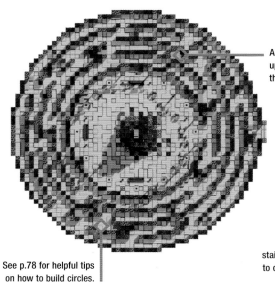

Add gift boxes to cheer up your friends when they take a wrong turn!

See p.78 for helpful tips on how to build circles.

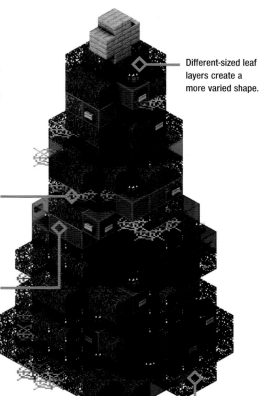

Different-sized leaf layers create a more varied shape.

Use cobwebs to create icicles and snowflakes.

Place blue and red stained glass diagonally to create a tinsel effect.

Start adding leaves three blocks above the floor to leave enough space for presents.

CENTER OF THE MAZE

Congratulations, you've made it to the center! Reward your friends for finishing the challenge with gifts under the tree and a carol concert of hits on the jukebox.

TRY THIS

Time how long it takes players to complete the maze. If your friends are struggling, make an easier maze with fewer layers that can be completed in under five minutes.

CRACKING UP

Have you ever opened a cracker and felt disappointed about what's inside? Well, that won't happen with a Minecraft cracker, because you get to build the contents yourself. You could even put a whole wintry scene inside if you like. This giant cracker opens with two levers to reveal a snug festive hideaway for players. Maybe that makes it a cozy cracker!

Add plants and mushrooms in the same colors as the cracker for added texture.

Place candles and magma blocks to light up the cracker.

Use fence gates, trapdoors, and stairs to create the uneven ends of the cracker.

BUILD TIP

To create the cracker shape, build two hollow 7x7x7 cubes for the ends and then create a longer cuboid with the same width for the middle part. Join them with a smaller 3x2x3 section made of stairs and slabs.

REDSTONE CIRCUIT

Crack open the piston door by pulling a lever on each side of the cracker. You'll need to pull both levers to open the door and get inside.

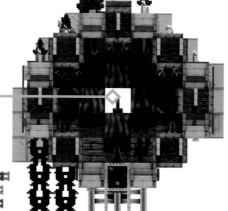

Challenge other players to get in the cracker by hiding the levers.

Build an opening door using two pistons, redstone, and two levers.

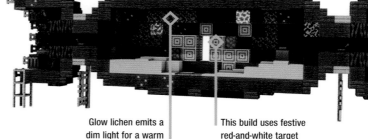

Add scaffolding so you can get to the levers.

HIDDEN HIDEOUT

If players can work out how to crack the cracker, they will be rewarded with a secret room. Fill it with valuable items and delicious treats.

Glow lichen emits a dim light for a warm atmosphere.

This build uses festive red-and-white target blocks for the door.

Decorate the side interiors with natural-looking hanging roots and pointed dripstone.

Store some delicious cakes inside your cracker to snack on.

TOWN SQUARE TRIP

This Minecraft town square radiates festive cheer, with every shopfront dazzlingly decorated for the holidays. Will passersby be tempted in for a last-minute purchase? Shutters, wonky chimneys, pitched roofs, and cobbled streets give a historic look to the square. It's a jolly old jumble, so pull everything together by stringing cobweb snowflake chains between the shops.

Top the roofs with snow for your town to feel like a real winter wonderland.

Fill a flower shop window with colorful plants to attract customers.

The trees in the town square are fully grown spruce trees.

Snowperson's arms are made using levers.

TRY THIS

To build a snowperson, place a snow block on top of a calcite block and set a carved pumpkin head on top. The calcite prevents it from transforming into a snow golem.

Overhang the upper floor by one or two blocks for a medieval-style building.

Create a central garden with short and tall grass, poppies, and dandelions.

FROSTY SHOP

Craft wonderfully wintry shops by building with ice. This frosty block makes a cheery blue shopfront that's sure to entice some very cool customers.

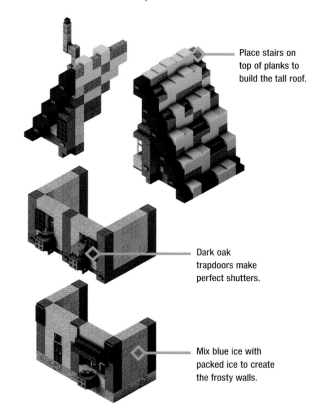

Place stairs on top of planks to build the tall roof.

Dark oak trapdoors make perfect shutters.

Mix blue ice with packed ice to create the frosty walls.

PRACTICAL PATHWAYS

Transform your town square with snow. Stack the layers as high as you want, but remember to leave clear pathways to the shops—or the shopkeepers won't be happy!

FESTIVE INTERIOR

Season's greetings! It might be cold outside, but this cozy interior is bursting with warmth and good cheer. What could be more festive than wooden beams, a flickering fire, and softly glowing candles? A Christmas tree takes pride of place in the corner, and the table is set with decorations. It's the perfect place to wish your Minecraft friends happy holidays.

Build a Christmas tree using leaves and spruce logs, or plant a tree on top of dirt, podzol, or grass.

Create a leafy garland to decorate the fireplace.

Add red banners to look like festive wall decorations.

TRY THIS

Pistons make a great alternative table. The piston head extends once placed on top of redstone blocks, torches, or levers. Add stairs for seating and decorate the table with candles.

Fill larger floor spaces by placing colorful carpet blocks to create a cozy rug.

CHRISTMAS TREE

A decorated festive tree is perfect for lighting up any room during the holidays. Build your own tree in Minecraft using spruce leaves and wooden logs.

FIREPLACE

Fireplaces add charm to any winter scene. Use bricks, stone bricks, and wooden logs to create the base of your fireplace before adding lots of intricate festive details.

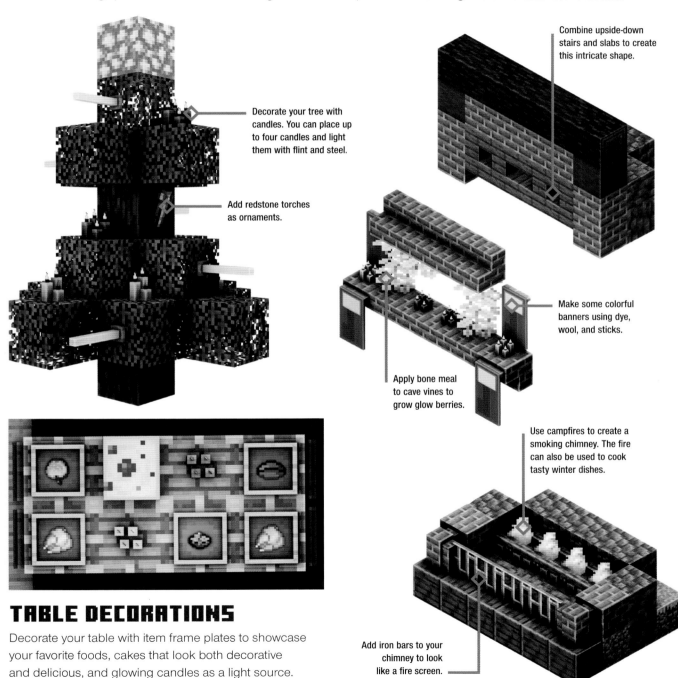

Combine upside-down stairs and slabs to create this intricate shape.

Decorate your tree with candles. You can place up to four candles and light them with flint and steel.

Add redstone torches as ornaments.

Make some colorful banners using dye, wool, and sticks.

Apply bone meal to cave vines to grow glow berries.

Use campfires to create a smoking chimney. The fire can also be used to cook tasty winter dishes.

TABLE DECORATIONS

Decorate your table with item frame plates to showcase your favorite foods, cakes that look both decorative and delicious, and glowing candles as a light source.

Add iron bars to your chimney to look like a fire screen.

SO MANY SNOWFLAKES

At this time of year, snowflakes are everywhere. You'll see them on greetings cards, wool sweaters, tree decorations, and maybe even in real life, too! Make a flurry of giant-sized snowflakes to decorate your Minecraft biomes. You can mix any colors you like and play around with sizes. These giant snowflakes use a lot of blocks, but they could be made even bigger.

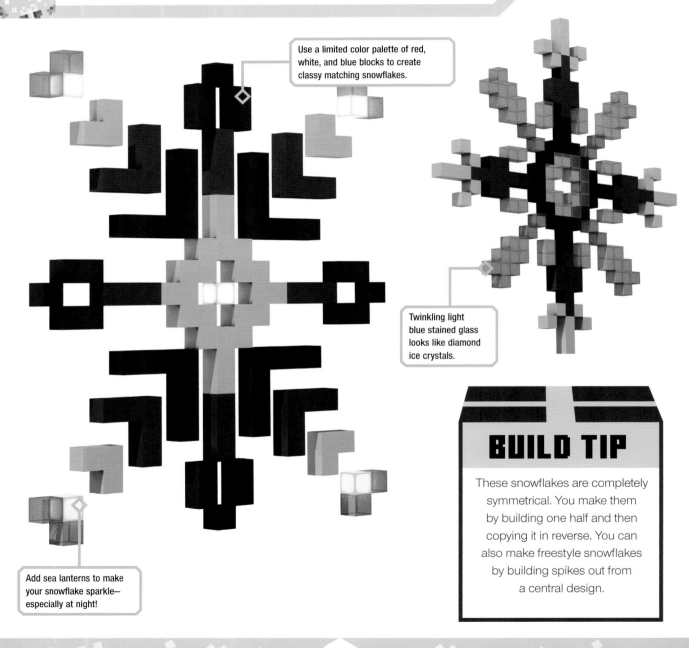

Use a limited color palette of red, white, and blue blocks to create classy matching snowflakes.

Twinkling light blue stained glass looks like diamond ice crystals.

Add sea lanterns to make your snowflake sparkle—especially at night!

BUILD TIP

These snowflakes are completely symmetrical. You make them by building one half and then copying it in reverse. You can also make freestyle snowflakes by building spikes out from a central design.

BY CANDLELIGHT

Count on candles to add a festive flicker to a holiday room! Make your Minecraft candles in vivid colors for a really jolly light show, and build them at different heights to give the impression they have burned unevenly. This cluster of candles is in an old-fashioned holder with a loop for carrying—just like one a Victorian (maybe even Scrooge) would have used.

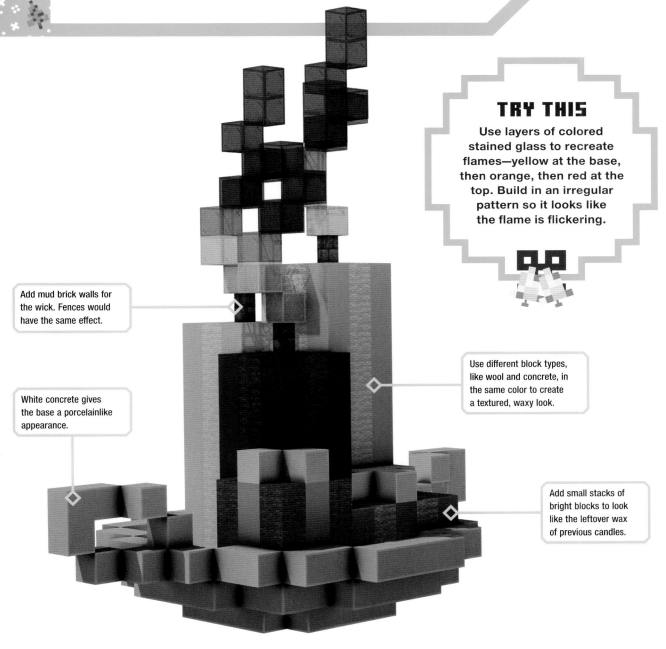

TRY THIS

Use layers of colored stained glass to recreate flames—yellow at the base, then orange, then red at the top. Build in an irregular pattern so it looks like the flame is flickering.

Add mud brick walls for the wick. Fences would have the same effect.

Use different block types, like wool and concrete, in the same color to create a textured, waxy look.

White concrete gives the base a porcelainlike appearance.

Add small stacks of bright blocks to look like the leftover wax of previous candles.

COZY WINTER CAFÉ

Don't leave players out in the cold! The striped roof of this cozy café will be a welcome sight to any wanderer in a snowy biome. Step inside for a drink and a slice of pumpkin pie, all served up by a gingerbread person. Add plenty of tables and warm End rod and lantern lighting to the café's interior for an atmosphere so comforting that customers might not want to leave.

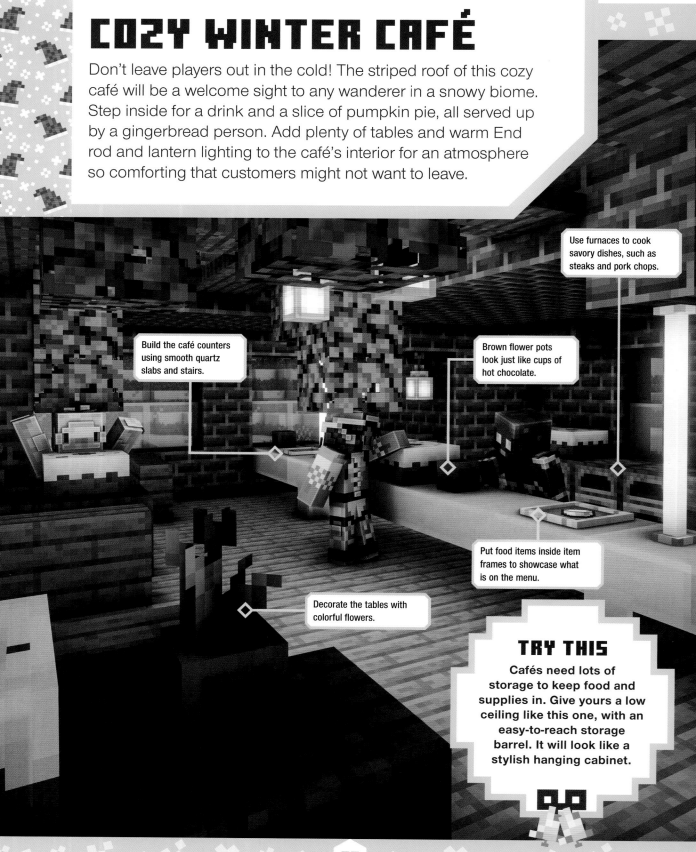

Use furnaces to cook savory dishes, such as steaks and pork chops.

Build the café counters using smooth quartz slabs and stairs.

Brown flower pots look just like cups of hot chocolate.

Put food items inside item frames to showcase what is on the menu.

Decorate the tables with colorful flowers.

TRY THIS

Cafés need lots of storage to keep food and supplies in. Give yours a low ceiling like this one, with an easy-to-reach storage barrel. It will look like a stylish hanging cabinet.

WELCOMING ENTRANCE

Entice people into your café by making the entrance area a cozy haven. Use bright colors and add plenty of flickering candles for a welcoming glow.

Build an awe-inspiring awning using red and white wool blocks.

Brick blocks give the café a solid-looking structure.

Add a floral display to the entrance using a decorated pot, a flower pot, and a cherry sapling.

TASTY TREATS

Indulge in a feast for your eyes and taste buds! The café offers delicious food to satisfy every craving, from cookies and cake to steak and pork chops. Wash your lunch down with a refreshing glass of milk. Yum!

OUTDOOR SEATING

Invite your friends to this café's charming seating area for a blend of tasty goods and snowy views. This veranda is built from fences and fence gates and has waxed oxidized cut copper flooring and a spruce slab roof.

CANDY CANE FOREST

At holiday time you'll see plenty of candy canes hanging on trees. This Minecraft build turns things around a bit. The candy canes *are* the trees! It's a whole candy cane forest for players to navigate, torch in hand. Stick to red and white stripes for a traditional peppermint cane look, and light the way with lanterns so players stay fine and dandy among the candy.

Combine two purpur stairs and one purpur slab to build this cute ribbon.

For a dense forest, add candy trees and candy canes in a variety of heights.

Decorate the forest paths with cherry wood fences.

TRY THIS

Set up a forest chase game. Split into two teams. One team sets off, leaving a trail of crumbs (cookies in item frames). After five minutes, the other team tries to find them, following the crumb clues.

Add a twist with a candy cane built from yellow terracotta and white concrete.

Light up your path with lanterns hanging off the canes and on fences.

Use packed mud that looks like chocolate to create paths.

CANDY TREE

This sweet forest is filled with candy trees alongside the giant candy canes. To build one, replace the trunk of a spruce tree with red terracotta and swap the leaves for red and white concrete blocks.

Add a light dusting of snow on the trees.

This tree is 10 blocks high.

Make the bottom layer of the tree the widest at seven blocks.

GIANT GIFTS

Add giant presents to mark locations throughout the forest. The boxes are made with glazed terracotta wrapping paper and the ribbons are made from colorful blocks.

Place stained glass panes around the sides and on the top to create ribbons.

Rotate glazed terracotta blocks to create different patterns on the wrapping paper.

CHUNKY CHALLENGE

Face your friends and family in a festive chunk challenge. Map out a single Minecraft chunk—that's 16 blocks wide by 16 blocks long—set a timer and see what you can build! This imaginative house features multiple floors, balconies, canopies, lanterns, and even an outdoor bench for players to admire the view, all in a small chunk-sized space.

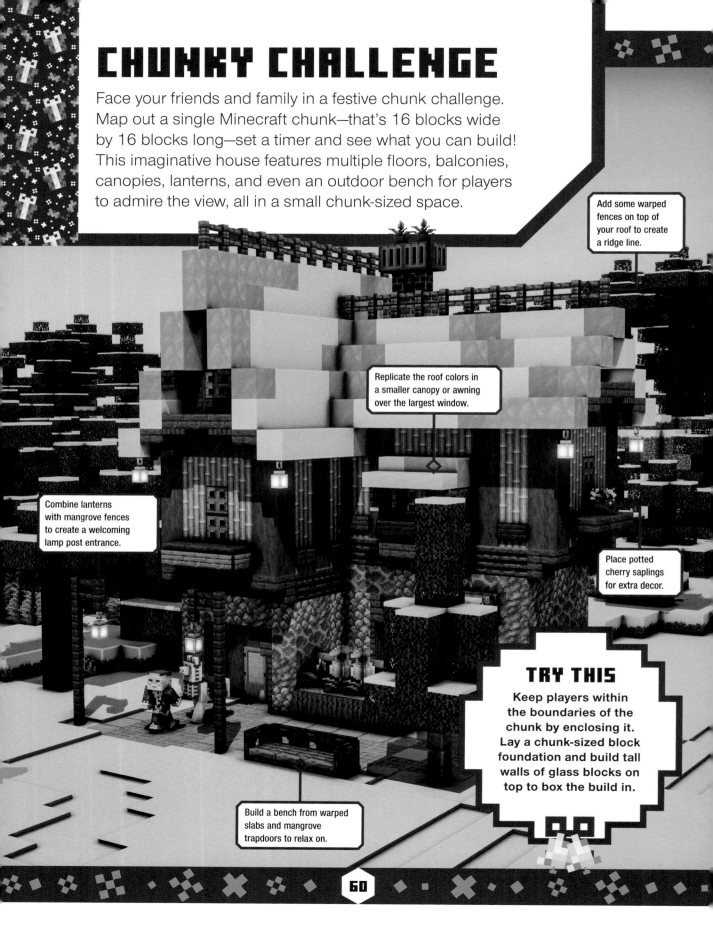

Add some warped fences on top of your roof to create a ridge line.

Replicate the roof colors in a smaller canopy or awning over the largest window.

Combine lanterns with mangrove fences to create a welcoming lamp post entrance.

Place potted cherry saplings for extra decor.

TRY THIS

Keep players within the boundaries of the chunk by enclosing it. Lay a chunk-sized block foundation and build tall walls of glass blocks on top to box the build in.

Build a bench from warped slabs and mangrove trapdoors to relax on.

BIG BUILD, SMALL SPACE

Start by building a 16x16 block base to place your build on and then let your creativity flow. You can create an awesome detailed house within this small area.

MATERIALS MATTER

Use a wide range of materials for your build to give it a big, bold look and impress other players. Consider using bright colors and contrasting textures.

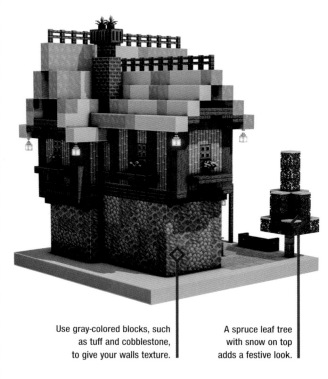

Use gray-colored blocks, such as tuff and cobblestone, to give your walls texture.

A spruce leaf tree with snow on top adds a festive look.

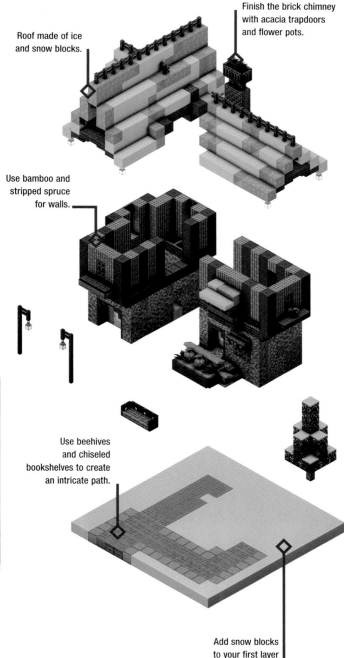

Roof made of ice and snow blocks.

Finish the brick chimney with acacia trapdoors and flower pots.

Use bamboo and stripped spruce for walls.

Use beehives and chiseled bookshelves to create an intricate path.

Add snow blocks to your first layer for a winter base.

STYLISH DETAILS

Pack the build with interesting details like a large door and window frames made from spruce trapdoors and stairs and a cute wooden flowerbed. Combine bamboo and stripped spruce logs for a colorful wall design.

ELF DOOR

Block block! Who's there? There could be anything behind this magical Minecraft door, deftly decorated by Santa's elves. Maybe even the elves themselves! This enchanting door is made from wooden planks and has a festive red-and-green border plus a robust-looking lock. Add a holly-wreathed porthole to your portal so the elves can peep in—or out!

Craft a red-and-white wool garland and decorate it with lanterns for a festive glow.

Decorate your entrance with an oak leaf wreath and garland.

Create fairy lights made of glass blocks and light-emitting blocks.

Build stockings made from concrete and terracotta.

Use red Nether brick slabs and walls for the wreath's bow.

Guide players to your door with a path made of snow blocks and snow layers.

BUILD TIP

Play around with the proportions of your builds. This door might look like a small elf entrance, but it's actually 26 blocks tall! Make giant grass using terracotta or concrete blocks to match the size of the door.

TOMTE NISSE

These cute gnomes come from Scandinavia, where they are linked to the festive season. They are said to protect people who respect them and punish people who don't. You'd better make a good job of your Minecraft tomte nisse, then! Give them handsome white beards, conical hats, and jolly lanterns to light their way through the forest at dusk.

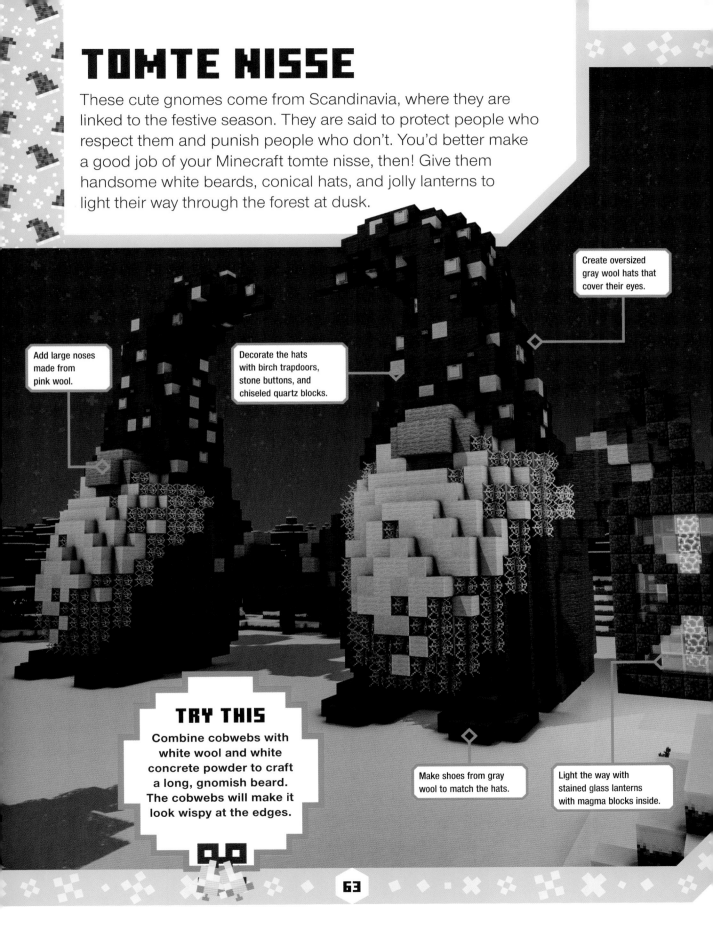

Create oversized gray wool hats that cover their eyes.

Add large noses made from pink wool.

Decorate the hats with birch trapdoors, stone buttons, and chiseled quartz blocks.

TRY THIS

Combine cobwebs with white wool and white concrete powder to craft a long, gnomish beard. The cobwebs will make it look wispy at the edges.

Make shoes from gray wool to match the hats.

Light the way with stained glass lanterns with magma blocks inside.

ICE HOTEL

Not everyone likes playing the host at holiday time. If you'd rather leave the catering to someone else, why not check into this fancy Minecraft ice hotel for a night of cold comfort? You'll get a frosty reception in this luxury lodge, but the rooms are spacious and offer a great view of the icy tundra landscape and beacon light show. Park your wolves outside and prepare to chill.

Construct a fancy domed roof from ice and packed ice for the main building.

Hide the beacons under snow. Only the glass panes that change the color of the beacons' light are visible.

A mini sleigh made of spruce trapdoors, signs, and slabs has arrived.

Create dramatic outdoor lamps by combining soul torches with dark oak fences.

BUILD TIP

For your beacon light show, build a 3x3 pyramid using iron blocks and place a beacon on top. Disable the beacon during the day with redstone. Use a sticky piston linked to a lever in the hotel to move one of the iron blocks and turn it on and off.

Add an elegant arched doorway using smooth quartz slabs.

Brighten up your hotel using colorful stained glass panes.

PERFECT PLANNING

Plan the layout of your hotel with a symmetrical design. This building has a reception at the center, a storage room at the back, and large bedrooms on either side. The bedrooms can fit eight guests (four on each side).

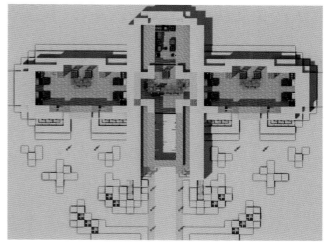

RELAXING BEDROOM

Decorate the hotel bedrooms with tables, chairs, and bookshelves. Items made from the colors and materials used on the exterior, such as this table made from light blue stained glass blocks, will create an elegant icy interior.

SNOW GLOBE

This glass globe on a base looks just like the decorative ones you shake to create a mini snowstorm. You might not be able to shake your Minecraft snow globe, but you can admire the scene you've created within. This globe contains a tiny tree and two candy canes, but yours could have a grand outdoor scene or a build of your favorite festive memory.

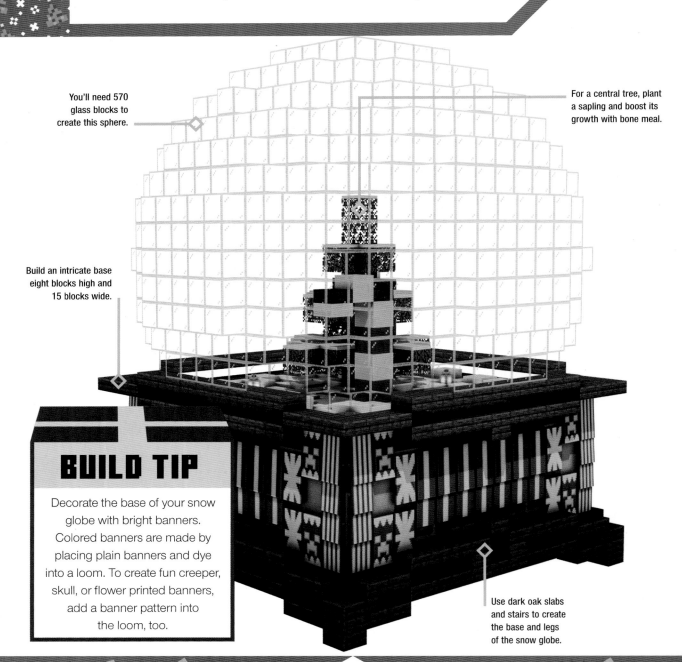

You'll need 570 glass blocks to create this sphere.

For a central tree, plant a sapling and boost its growth with bone meal.

Build an intricate base eight blocks high and 15 blocks wide.

BUILD TIP

Decorate the base of your snow globe with bright banners. Colored banners are made by placing plain banners and dye into a loom. To create fun creeper, skull, or flower printed banners, add a banner pattern into the loom, too.

Use dark oak slabs and stairs to create the base and legs of the snow globe.

ICE MOB STATUES

Did someone say freeze? These Minecraft mobs are frozen to the spot! Build your own statues based on hostile zombie, creeper, spider, and skeleton mobs and cover them with a thick layer of ice. Thankfully, these chilly creations are as still as a statue, so they can't do any damage, but they're still very cool.

Add ice blocks to give the mobs a wintry look.

Classic zombie shirt is made from cyan wool and concrete.

Combine blue wool and concrete to make pants.

Build a creeper using concrete and green and lime terracotta.

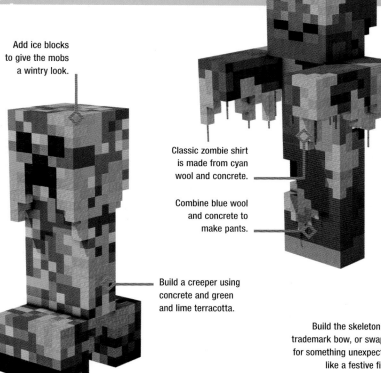

TRY THIS

Challenge yourself to catch a mob in Survival mode to use as a reference for your statue. Alternatively, you can use a spawn egg in Creative mode to generate a mob.

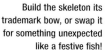

Build the skeleton its trademark bow, or swap it for something unexpected like a festive fish!

Build a sturdy spider's body from blackstone, basalt, and deepslate.

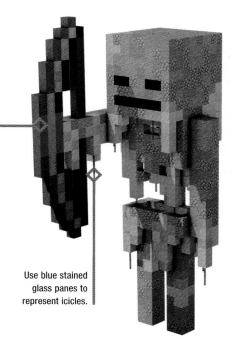

Use blue stained glass panes to represent icicles.

Use deepslate, redstone ore, and black glazed terracotta for the spider's sinister eyes.

HOUSE OF LIGHTS

Let it glow, let it glow, let it glow! The residents of this house won't be outshone at holiday time. They've gone completely over the top with their display of festive lights. Lanterns, froglights, and shroomlights glow out from all sides, and there's even a campfire in the front garden. This brilliant build has the maximum impact against a dark, starry night sky.

TRY THIS

Design a whole house using shroomlights as the main building material. The bright build wouldn't need any extra decorations or lights to stand out in a dark winter night.

The night is full of hostile mobs, like this sneaky skeleton.

Decorate your garden with candy canes made from red and white blocks.

Walls made of dark oak trapdoors contrast against the snowy landscape.

Light up your roof with glowing shroomlights. The light reflects off the shiny red glazed terracotta.

This house uses different types of wood, like this birch stairs balcony.

FROGLIGHTS

Make your build dazzle with giant froglight baubles. Use a chain to easily attach them to the house for subtle color and illumination.

Vary the length of the chain to dangle the bauble higher or lower.

Froglights come in three colors: pearlescent, verdant, and ocher.

BRIGHT WINDOWS

Place froglights behind the window panes to create a warm, festive glow within the house. These will look great to players seeing them from the outside, but they'll obscure the view for those inside!

SAUNA AND SPA

Winter breaks don't have to involve snowball fights and ice skating. This festive spa is perfect for players who would rather relax their way into a happy new Minecraft year. There's a tranquil hot tub to soak in and lounge chairs to have a nap on ... ahhhhh. At the back, a steamy sauna room with a tub of sizzling coals awaits. It's perfect for melting away any winter worries!

Sauna is visible behind a glass pane window.

Surround your pool with windows for views of the winter wonderland outside.

Use snow layers to vary the height of the lounge chairs. Eight snow layers are equal to one block.

Add quartz and prismarine stairs for easy access to the hot tub.

Use the tops of chiseled bookshelves to create a unique floor texture.

TRY THIS

This spa uses quartz for a clean, modern look. For a twist, build a Roman spa using sandstone variants. It could have a grand Roman bath surrounded by tall sandstone pillars.

SAUNA CABIN

Sitting in a toasty sauna can be relaxing, especially when it's cold outside. Make your own sauna cabin with spruce plank walls, then add a magma block to heat up the room.

COZY BENCH

It can get very hot in a sauna, so it's important to have a place to sit down. Build a sauna bench using spruce trapdoors. Add two levels to the bench to fit on more people.

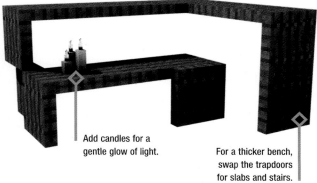

Add candles for a gentle glow of light.

For a thicker bench, swap the trapdoors for slabs and stairs.

FINISHING TOUCHES

Add decorations to the spa that will make players feel relaxed. Bring nature indoors with a few plants, and don't forget hydration with a water dispenser, too!

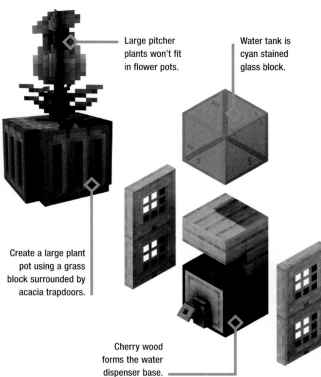

Large pitcher plants won't fit in flower pots.

Water tank is cyan stained glass block.

Create a large plant pot using a grass block surrounded by acacia trapdoors.

Cherry wood forms the water dispenser base.

BUBBLE POOL

Treat your spa guests to a bubbling hot tub. Use soul sand for the base of the pool, then build the sides using quartz. Add the water, hop in, and relax in a sea of bubbles.

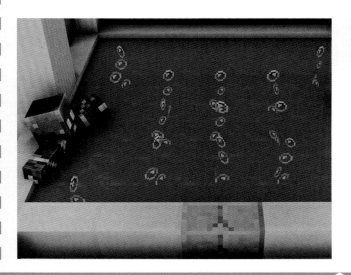

WITCH'S HOLIDAY HUT

Upgrade a witch's home from a swamp hut to a cozy winter hideaway with a magical twist. That's not soup bubbling in the cauldron; it's a brewing potion. Those aren't carol books on the shelves; they're spell books. For a finishing touch, add festive bunting and fairy lights so this winter witch and their cat can celebrate the holidays.

Connect five crimson hanging signs to create bunting.

Grow cave vines to yield glow berries and light up the hut with a gentle glow.

Hide magical gifts for the witch in this chest—and some fish for the cat!

Add a lectern to hold a spell book filled with potion recipes.

Match the carpet to the bunting for a cohesive look.

HOT COCOA HEAVEN

Winter weather can be really bitter. What you need is something sweet. Come in from the cold and make yourself a hot drink—a real one and a matching Minecraft one, too. These striped Minecraft mugs are chock-full of hot chocolatey details. Add floating marshmallows, candy canes, and a stirring spoon to your block-built mugs of steaming cocoa, and relax!

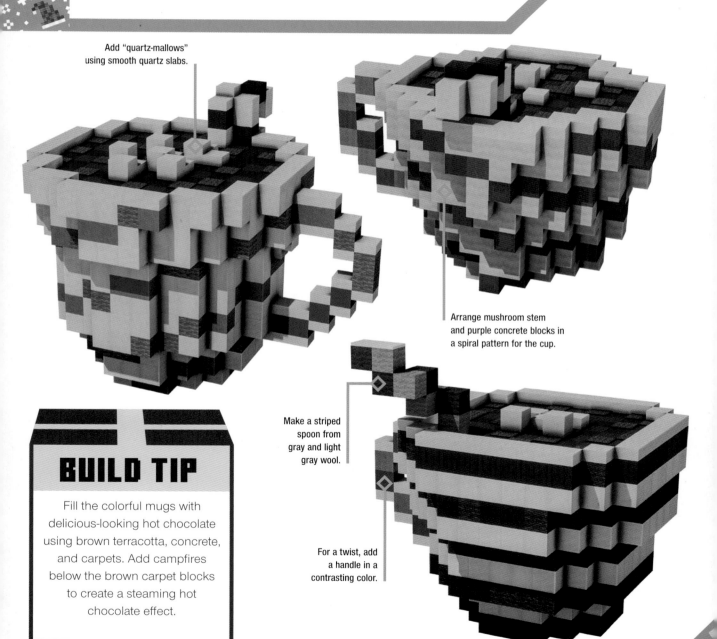

Add "quartz-mallows" using smooth quartz slabs.

Arrange mushroom stem and purple concrete blocks in a spiral pattern for the cup.

Make a striped spoon from gray and light gray wool.

For a twist, add a handle in a contrasting color.

BUILD TIP

Fill the colorful mugs with delicious-looking hot chocolate using brown terracotta, concrete, and carpets. Add campfires below the brown carpet blocks to create a steaming hot chocolate effect.

ICE RINK ANTICS

Ready for some winter-themed fun? This game will provide plenty of hijinks in the ice rink. Players board boats on the rink and throw snowballs at other boats, trying their best to hit them and cause the boat to vanish. Watch out for the spectators hurling snowballs, too! Call your friends to get on the ice and fight it out to be the last boat on the rink.

Make a barrier from crimson planks so the boats don't accidentally leave the ice.

Build stalls where players can get their boats and snowballs.

TRY THIS

Build your rink using blue ice instead of regular ice. The boats will go significantly faster on a blue ice rink, and it won't melt under bright light sources.

Remember, your ice rink can be any shape—long, wide, narrow, or irregular.

Add lots of bright lights so that everyone can see the action.

Santa's boat has been hit!

SUPPLY STALLS

Keep players well supplied by adding a small stall with boats and snowballs for them to use in the game. Build the stall's frame with cherry wood and jungle fences.

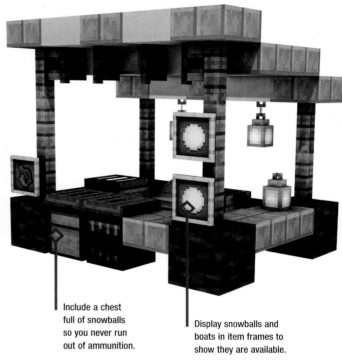

Include a chest full of snowballs so you never run out of ammunition.

Display snowballs and boats in item frames to show they are available.

PERFECT PERGOLA

This ice rink is covered by a pergola, a wooden garden feature that keeps the worst of the snow off spectators. Experiment with fences, trapdoors, and gates to create the pergola frame and attach lanterns and froglights for lighting.

WINTER BOAT FLUME

This winter boat flume ride gives Santa's sleigh a run for its money. In fact, for anyone afraid of heights, it could be more "Oh oh oh!" than "Ho ho ho!" The festive flume whooshes passengers down a steep water flume to an icy splashdown at the bottom. Build the launch hut high—players boarding the boats must be prepared for a really chilling drop.

TRY THIS

Add a boat dispenser to the hut at the top of the flume to generate boats. Make sure the dispenser is in the water so the boats will shoot out, ready for players to ride.

Four end rods around a white stained glass block make a cool roof decoration.

A polished andesite path leads you to the slide.

Stop ice from forming by filling the pool's floor with glowstone blocks.

Place trapdoors around the edge of the pool to look like the pool's gutter.

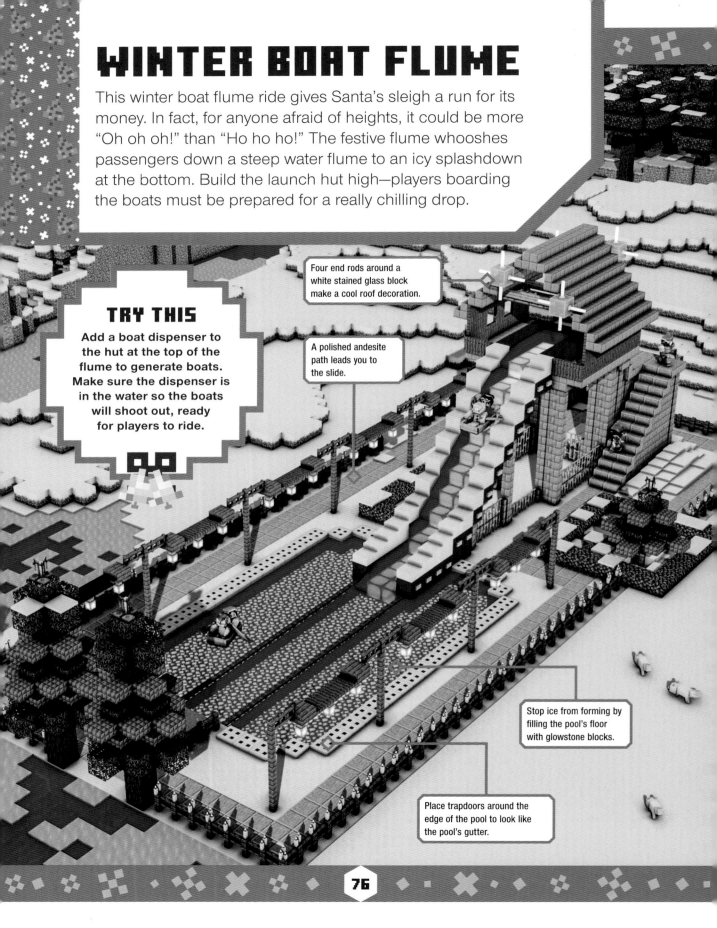

SPEEDY SLIDE

Build a slide for players to ride their boats down—it can be a nice, evenly stepped slide like this one, or it can include dramatic drops. Remember to stop water from turning into ice to prevent icy surprises.

Construct a roof from copper stairs so you can shelter from the winter weather.

Include sea lanterns underneath the slide to prevent the water from freezing.

Stack layers of snow to make the sides of your slide.

SMALL FIR TREE

Make your build look merry by including a cute little festive tree! Place layers of slabs for branches, then add leaves to soften the shape and add texture.

Top your tree with a brewing stand.

Use thin dark prismarine slabs instead of blocks to keep the tree tiny.

FROSTY POOL FUN

Build lanes made of mangrove hanging signs for your frosty pool to separate the boats. Some lanes are for players rushing down the flume and others are for those enjoying a casual paddle.

LEAFY WREATHS

A wreath on the door is a great way to tell people you're celebrating the winter season. Red and green are popular festive colors, but you can use any color combinations you like! Green blocks and leaves can represent holly and ivy, but did you know there is another festive plant that has bright red foliage? It's called a poinsettia.

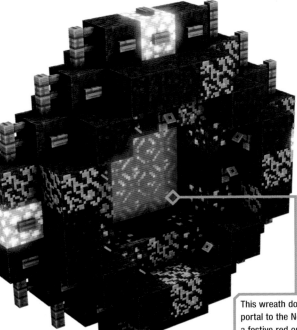

Place diamond, gold, and redstone blocks in item frames to make colorful baubles for the wreath.

End rods emit white particles that look like snow.

This wreath doubles as a portal to the Nether and a festive red ornament.

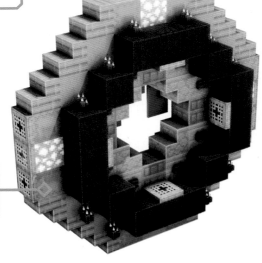

BUILD TIP

Build a perfect circle in Minecraft by planning it on graph paper first. Place a compass in the middle of a square and draw a circle. Then color in each square that the circle touches. Use this blueprint to build a circle, or wreath, with Minecraft blocks.

Use materials in different colors and textures, like bamboo and birch stairs, to add variety to your wreath.

ALL WRAPPED UP

Make this tantalizing collection of seasonal presents and you'll really have gift-giving covered. Plain or patterned, large or small, your presents should hint at wonderful things inside. Add a chest to fill with the perfect Minecraft gifts for your friends and family, and decorate the presents with some ribbons and bows if you want to be a bit fancy.

Add upside-down smooth quartz stairs as the present's ribbon.

TOP TIP

If you usually put your gifts underneath a Christmas tree, look for a spruce tree in a snowy biome to recreate the experience in Minecraft.

Surround chests with trapdoors to make them look like nicely wrapped presents.

Decorate your presents with buttons and objects in item frames.

Use coral blocks for colorful presents. Place them on top of a block of water to keep the coral bright and alive.

WOLF SLEIGH

Santa's giving his reindeer a break this year, but Minecraft villagers can still hear sleigh bells jing-jing-jingling. Four kindly wolves have offered to pull Santa's sleigh. Unfortunately, they're more Gnasher and Cruncher than Dasher and Dancer, so they've been distracted by the smell of roast meat and let the sleigh grind to a halt. Will those presents ever be delivered?

Add glazed terracotta blocks to look like simple presents.

Recreate sleigh runners using bamboo trapdoors.

Add bamboo fence gates to the front of your runners to give them a rounded appearance.

BUILD TIP

Make sure you build your sleigh on snow and then create realistic sleigh tracks by digging up the snow layer behind and underneath. This will make it look like your sleigh has been on the move!

Use a leash on a wolf to guide it or tether it to objects like fence posts.

SANTA'S SLEIGH

Need extra gift capacity? Build two sleighs and link them together using fence gates or chains for a double dose of presents.

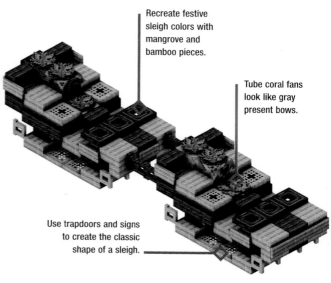

Recreate festive sleigh colors with mangrove and bamboo pieces.

Tube coral fans look like gray present bows.

Use trapdoors and signs to create the classic shape of a sleigh.

Wolves aren't the only tameable mobs— how about a sleigh pulled by parrots or cats?

Untamed wolves are missing a collar.

FESTIVE FRIEND

Tame a wolf by giving it bones until hearts appear. Keep your loyal companion happy by feeding it a steady diet of meat.

SNUG SKI CHALET

Ski-daddle your way to a snowy biome and get building this snug ski chalet. Nestling at the bottom of the slopes, it has a wide, pitched roof with overhanging eaves. Top yours off with snow—several layers will suggest that conditions are ideal for skiing. Players back from their downhill dash can tuck themselves up in the chalet's cozy living room for an after-ski chat.

Refine your chalet with added details like unlit campfires and buttons.

Make a realistic roof by stacking snow layers to look like there has been a heavy snowfall.

Add a planter with grass blocks and a pretty cherry sapling for a splash of color.

TRY THIS

Make good use of the overhanging roof—it provides good shelter from the snow. You could add a rustic patio underneath with tables, chairs, and potted plants.

Use natural-looking spruce and dark oak variants for the roof of the chalet.

Place spruce logs in a pile secured by rails to look like freshly chopped wood.

UNUSUAL INVENTORY

Enhance the walls and roofs by using unconventional blocks, like looms and smokers. See what unexpected textures and patterns you can create.

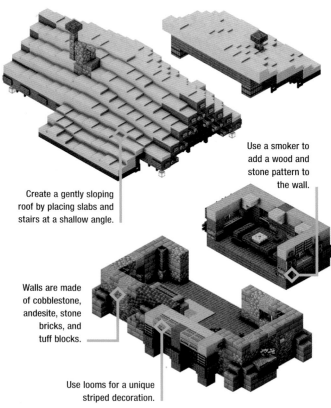

Use a smoker to add a wood and stone pattern to the wall.

Create a gently sloping roof by placing slabs and stairs at a shallow angle.

Walls are made of cobblestone, andesite, stone bricks, and tuff blocks.

Use looms for a unique striped decoration.

STAYING SNUG

Give your ski chalet a warm and welcoming interior. Include an open fire, a large cyan and light blue carpet rug, and comfy cherry stair seating. Then sit back and enjoy the chilly views from inside your super-snug space.

CHIMNEY VINE

Have you ever wondered how Santa gets down the chimney? This Minecraft fireplace gives the secret away: He clambers down a vine (no doubt wearing boots with Fire Resistance). Surround your fireplace with candles, ornaments, and item frames for a traditional look. Don't forget to leave some cookies and milk on the table—delivering presents makes Santa hungry!

TRY THIS

Make the room at least five blocks tall so it's big enough to fit in this detailed chimney scene. You'll need three blocks for the fireplace, plus extra room for the decorations on top.

Use green and lime terracotta blocks to create cozy living room walls.

Decorate your mantelpiece with flower pots, candles, and a bell.

This enchantment table can be used as decoration and as a useful way to enchant presents.

Make a simple table with two bamboo trapdoors for the legs and a birch trapdoor for the top.

ITEM FRAME DECOR

Create simple, effective decorations by using item frames. While Santa can't place gifts in the stockings (boots in an item frame), he might swap them for a new item or enchant them.

CLASSIC FIREPLACE

You can't go wrong with a classic brick fireplace. Add a creative flair by playing with the orientation of your bricks to create interesting shapes and patterns.

CHIMNEY CHAMBER

Add a one block wide chamber lined with calcite blocks behind the fireplace. This will house the twisting vine Santa uses to shimmy down the chimney.

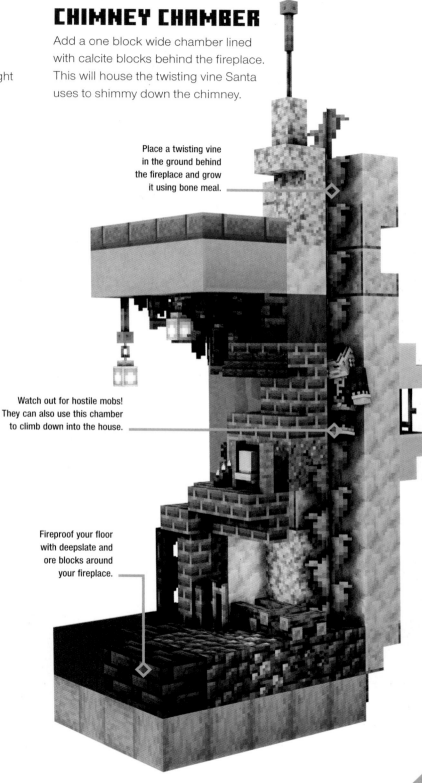

Place a twisting vine in the ground behind the fireplace and grow it using bone meal.

Watch out for hostile mobs! They can also use this chamber to climb down into the house.

Fireproof your floor with deepslate and ore blocks around your fireplace.

GINGERBREAD HOUSE

This Minecraft house really is a home sweet home—with the emphasis on sweet! It's constructed from blocks that look like smooth white icing and sticky gingerbread. Base your build on the gingerbread houses sold in stores at holiday time. Next, spice it up with colorful candles on the roof. When it's ready, invite some players to visit. Smart cookies only!

Use soul soil and mud bricks to create delicious-looking gingerbread and chocolate roof tiles.

Recreate gummy sweet decorations with weeping vines.

Add lots of candles to recreate multicolored sprinkles.

Target blocks look like tasty frosting.

TRY THIS

Sweeten up your gingerbread garden by adding a chocolate fountain. Use brown stained glass and glass panes for the chocolate and a smooth quartz block for the fountain.

SWEET HOME

This build is all about using common blocks like wood and mud in clever and different ways to recreate the mouthwatering look of a gingerbread house in Minecraft.

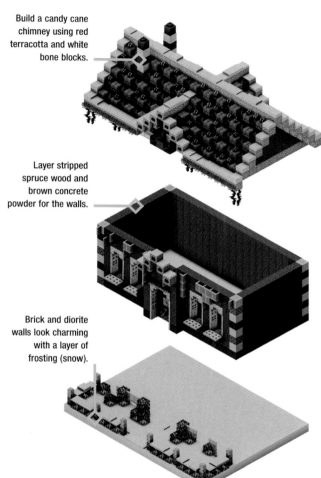

Build a candy cane chimney using red terracotta and white bone blocks.

Layer stripped spruce wood and brown concrete powder for the walls.

Brick and diorite walls look charming with a layer of frosting (snow).

OUTER LAYERS

Build doors and windows with two layers for a more complex build. This window's outer frame is in front and the sash is in the backdrop.

This window area is five blocks tall and four blocks wide.

Use iron doors to create sugarlike window frames.

ELYTRA ELF COURSE

Can elves fly? Santa might chuckle at the idea, but in Minecraft, they definitely can. They just have to find an End ship, grab some elytra wings, and hit the skies. Build a mountainous Minecraft obstacle course and give you and your elf friends a challenge. The first one to fly through every ring will become the elf-proclaimed champion of the course.

Build a tower at the highest point of your course. This is where the race starts!

TRY THIS

You don't have to build the terrain for your elytra elf course. Find a stony peaks or eroded badlands biome and set up your course there. Save your time for the epic test flights!

Craft simple rings using 16 blocks made of concrete and glowing shroomlights.

Connect the islands using a simple mud brick bridge.

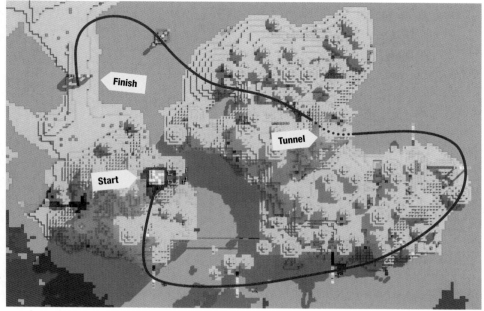

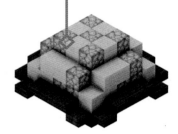

Build the tower's roof using white wool and shroomlights.

BIRD'S-EYE VIEW

Map out the obstacle course from the sky. Fly high above the terrain (either using elytra wings or in Creative mode) to get an overview of the land. From here, you can see where to start and which mountains to fly around and can plot the course.

Leave a gap in the platform's bamboo fence barrier so you can easily jump off—and fly!

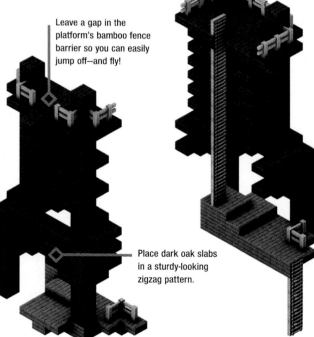

Place dark oak slabs in a sturdy-looking zigzag pattern.

FLY GEAR

Unlock the exhilarating experience of flight in Survival mode! To get an elytra, venture to the End dimension, defeat the Ender Dragon, and explore the End cities to find an End ship and this amazing winged accessory.

TALL TOWER

A tall tower is the perfect place to start the race. Not only are the views amazing, but the higher you are, the easier it is for you to take off and swoop through the rings to victory. Ready, steady ... GO!

ADDING OBSTACLES

If you want to tackle the trickiest of trials, build your course with lots of obstacles to dodge. Add a forest full of trees, some very sharp bends, and a treacherous cave to give you and your friends a super-fun challenge. Practice makes perfect!

Add bamboo trapdoors to your ladder for a more unique look.

Place the rings at different angles to add an exciting challenge.

Don't build the rings too far apart. Players need to see the next ring to fly to.

Use bright blocks for the final ring—instead of redstone lamps, you could use netherrack and light it up for a blazing finish!

CAVE DIVE

Add a creepy cave section in your elytra course. Players will need to navigate thrilling dives, twists, and turns as they avoid the pointed dripstone obstacles and spruce fences from old mineshafts.

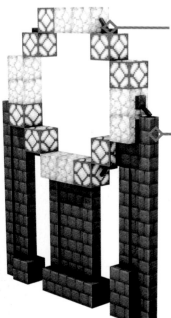

You don't need to attach levers directly to the lamps to turn them on and off.

Place the final ring on a mud brick wall podium.

THE FINISH

Enhance the visibility of the final ring by adding redstone lamps. Whiz through the ring first to become the elytra elf course champion.

GLOSSARY

Jumping into the world of Minecraft will introduce you to lots of new terms. Here, you'll find a list of some of the terms that appear in the book and what they mean in Minecraft.

BANNER

A tall, decorative block that can be dyed and designed on a loom.

BEACON

A block that projects a beam of light. To work, a beacon must be placed on a pyramid base made of iron, gold, diamond, emerald, or Netherite blocks.

BIOME

A unique landscape in Minecraft, such as ocean, plains, and swamp biomes. There are more than 60 biomes in Minecraft.

BLOCK

A basic unit of structure in Minecraft occupying one unit of space.

BOOK

An item crafted with leather and paper. It can be written in or used for enchanting.

BUTTON

An interactive block that sends a redstone signal when pushed.

CARPET

A thin, flat layer of wool that can be dyed up to 16 colors.

CRAFTING TABLE

A utility block used by Survival players to craft blocks.

CREATIVE MODE

A game mode that gives players access to an infinite supply of Minecraft's blocks and the ability to fly.

CREEPER

A hostile mob that explodes when near players.

ELYTRA

A pair of wings that can be found in the End dimension. Players can use it to glide through the air.

ENCHANTING TABLE

An interactive block that can be used to enchant items using experience and lapis lazuli.

ENCHANTMENT

An enhancement that can be added to a tool to improve its utility.

THE END

A dark dimension in Minecraft, characterized by the presence of the Ender Dragon and strange terrain.

END CITY

A city found on the outer islands of the End. Usually located next to an End ship.

END ROD

A naturally generated light source that can also be used for decoration, to climb towers, or to melt snow and ice.

FENCE

A barrier block with openings that players can see through, unlike a wall. Usually, a fence cannot be jumped over.

FIRE RESISTANCE

A status that grants the player or mob immunity to sources of fire damage, such as fire, lava, and magma blocks.

ITEM

One of many types of objects in a player's inventory. When an item is used, a block or other entity (such as a minecart or boat) appears in the game. Items can only be displayed within the game in an item frame, a glow item frame, or an armor stand.

LIGHT SOURCE

A light-emitting block, such as a torch, a lantern, a froglight, or a campfire.

MINECART

A trainlike vehicle that can only be placed on a rail. Minecarts can be ridden but will stop if anything gets in their way.

MOB

A computer-controlled entity that behaves like a living creature. Mobs can be neutral, passive, or hostile.

THE NETHER

An inhospitable dimension in Minecraft.

THE OVERWORLD

A dimension in Minecraft with diverse biomes. The starting place of a player.

PISTON

A block capable of moving items, blocks, and players when given a redstone signal.

PRESSURE PLATE

A block that can produce a redstone signal when stood on.

REDSTONE

A general term for Minecraft's engineering blocks and system that allow players tocreate machines and add functioning devices to their builds.

SHULKER BOX

A block that can store items and be dyed. It keeps its contents in item form when broken.

SLABS

A decorative block variant that is half the height of a block.

SMELT

A method of refining blocks in Survival mode. For example, smelting will change iron ores into iron ingots.

SNOW GOLEM

A passive mob made of two snow blocks and a carved pumpkin.

SOUL SAND

A block found in the Nether and ancient cities. It is used in creating bubbles and soul campfires.

SPAWN

The creation of mobs and players in the game.

STAIRS

A stepped decorative block variant.

SURVIVAL MODE

A game mode where players must collect their resources and survive the dangers of day and night.

TRAPDOOR

An interactive barrier block that can be opened and closed with a redstone signal or by hand.

VARIANT

A variation of a basic block. These include slabs, stairs, walls, trapdoors, buttons, and chiseled blocks.

VILLAGER

A passive mob that interacts with players by offering trades.

WITHER

A hostile mob that can hover and fire explosive skulls at targets.

STAYING SAFE ONLINE

It's fun to use the internet to play games, watch videos, or communicate with others, but it's important to stay safe. Here are some guidelines to follow to keep you safe when spending time online.

- Always use a username when posting something or chatting with others online (and make sure it doesn't contain your real name).

- Never give out personal information such as your name, how old you are, your phone number, or where you live.

- Never tell anyone the name or location of your school.

- Never share your password or login information with anyone (except with a parent or guardian).

- Never send personal photos to anyone.

- Always get your parent's or guardian's permission if you decide to create an account online (and remember that on many websites, you need to be 13 or older to do this).

- Always tell a trusted adult if anything online has made you feel worried or uncomfortable.